Fenced Off:
The Suburbanization of
American Politics

Juliet F. Gainsborough

GEORGETOWN UNIVERSITY PRESS / WASHINGTON, D.C.

Georgetown University Press, Washington, D.C.
©2001 by Georgetown University Press. All rights reserved.
Printed in the United States of America

10 9 8 7 6 5 4 3 2 1   2001

Library of Congress Cataloguing in Publication Data

Gainsborough, Juliet F.
   Fenced off: the suburbanization of American politics / by Juliet
Gainsborough.
   p. cm.—(American governance and public policy series)
Includes bibliographical references and index.
ISBN 0-87840-830-4 (cloth : alk. paper)—ISBN 0-87840-831-2 (pbk. : alk.
paper) 1. Political participation—United States. 2. Suburbs—Political
aspects—United States. I. Title. II. American governance and public policy.

JK1764.G65 2001
306.2'0973'091733—dc21   00-061019

To my parents, John and Jenni Gainsborough

Contents

Preface

From "angry white males" to "soccer moms," talk of the suburban voter has dominated much of the popular political commentary of the last several election cycles. However, while suburbanization received attention from academics during the 1950s and 1960s, very little recent work has been done on the topic. This book is an attempt to use some of the tools of political science to explore an argument that seems self-evident to many political observers: place matters.

My interest in place developed naturally, out of my own varied experiences of place—growing up in England; attending high school in Los Angeles, college in Berkeley, graduate school in Boston; and visiting my parents in their new home of Washington, D.C. The intersection between place and politics was sharply illustrated for me when I moved from the predominantly Republican suburb of Santa Clarita to the decidedly left-of-center city of Berkeley. And this sense of the importance of place was crystallized by the experience of writing a senior thesis exploring Santa Clarita's incorporation campaign. For encouraging me in this endeavor and in the subsequent decision to go to graduate school, I have Sandy Muir to thank. Among other comments on my thesis, he included the remark that I would surely draw on these ideas for many years to come; how right he was.

This is only the first of many intellectual and personal debts incurred along the way as my interest in the politics of place moved from research paper to dissertation to book. Paul Peterson, Sidney Verba, and Bradley Palmquist all read drafts of each chapter and offered important feedback and criticism. They also provided useful professional advice at crucial moments. In particular, I am indebted to Paul Peterson for well-timed words of encouragement.

I was especially fortunate at Harvard to meet a remarkable group of fellow graduate students, without whose friendship this book would never have been completed. In particular, Sini Gandhi, Pat Joyce, Eric Thun, and Karissa Price helped me shape the original idea into dissertation form and sustained me through the years with invaluable and uncountable talks, laughs, and cups of coffee. Sini even came up with the idea of using "fenced off" for the title. My luck in finding col-

viii   Fenced Off: The Suburbanization of American Politics

leagues has followed me to my new home at the University of Miami, where the process of turning dissertation into book was completed. Special thanks for his support during this stage of the process go to Tom Sloan.

Finally, a huge thank you is owed to my parents, John and Jenni Gainsborough. Without their love and support, none of the good things in my life would have been possible. By encouraging the exploration of ideas and the pursuit of new experiences, they have truly been the sparks for my academic endeavors. And, by always providing a safe haven, they have made even the scariest undertakings manageable.

CHAPTER ONE

Suburban Myths Then and Now: Camptown and Arroyo Blanco

In 1949, Charles Mergendahl's novel *It's Only Temporary* finds Donald and Shelley Cousins and their three-year-old daughter moving into Camptown, a new town within commuting distance of New York City.[1] The community consists of 4,000 houses—the outsides of which "varied slightly, as there were seven distinct models. Inside they were precisely alike."[2] The streets, named after fish or animals, are so difficult to tell apart that on the day that his wife and daughter arrive, Donald circles past his new home twice before finally locating it. At first Donald and Shelley are appalled by the sameness of the homes and by the conformity of their neighbors' lives—the men who carpool together to the train station to boring jobs in New York and return to Camptown on the same train every evening, and the wives who shop together and compete over who buys better groceries or nicer dresses. Slowly, however, the Cousins start to settle into their Camptown lives: becoming friends with their neighbors, adding a picket fence and arborvitae bushes to their home—and, finally, postponing Donald's dream of entrepreneurship in Montana for the prospect of a promotion at his insurance company's New York office.

T. Coraghessan Boyle's novel *The Tortilla Curtain*, set in the early 1990s, finds Delaney Mossbacher, his second wife, Kyra, and her six-year-old son living in a housing development in the hills of Los Angeles. Although the homes are larger and more expensive, they are, like those of Camptown, nearly identical to each other. Instead of being named after animals and fish, the streets are all named *Via* and *Calle* and *Avenida,* and the houses are "all of the Spanish Mission style, painted in one of three prescribed shades of white, with orange roofs. If you wanted to paint your house sky-blue or Provençal-pink with lime-green shutters, you were perfectly welcome to move into the San Fernando Valley or to Santa Monica or anywhere else you chose, but if you bought into Arroyo Blanco Estates, your house would be white and your roof orange."[3]

Like the Cousins in Camptown, Delaney and his wife at first resist, but ultimately embrace, the values of the other members of their community. Though he had initially objected to the idea of placing a gate and guard at the entrance to the housing estate, Delaney changes his mind after unpleasant encounters with illegal immigrants who are camped in the canyon below his home leave him feeling threatened and insecure. His wife, traumatized by her own run-in with Mexican immigrants and the loss of two of her dogs to a coyote, takes the desire for protection one step further and campaigns for the construction of a wall around the entire Arroyo Blanco Estates.

What do these two fictional portraits of suburban living, separated as they are by more than forty years, have to tell us? First, the notion that suburban living has the power to affect attitudes and behavior is not a new one. And despite the best efforts of sociologists and political scientists to debunk the suburban myths of the 1950s—which held that moving to the suburbs transformed residents into isolated conformists who voted for the Republican Party—the belief persists that the movement to the suburbs has profound implications for modern society.

Second, despite the many parallels between Camptown and Arroyo Blanco Estates, the pictures of suburban living offered by these novels differ in important ways. For the Cousins and their neighbors, living in Camptown represents the attainment of the American middle-class dream—and their concerns, once there, center on being able to keep up with the neighbors in terms of home improvement and career advancement. The Camptown residents are not fearful of the city—in fact, they work there, and dine there on wedding anniversaries—but the city is just not where people who want to own their own homes and raise their children choose to live. For the residents of Arroyo Blanco, however, the housing estate represents not merely status but escape. After a coyote carries off one of his wife's dogs, Delaney reflects: "Nature was the least of their problems. It was humans they were worried about. The Salvadorans, the Mexicans, the blacks, the gangbangers and taggers and carjackers they read about in the Metro section over their bran toast and coffee. That's why they'd abandoned the flatlands of the Valley and the hills of the Westside to live up here, outside the city limits, in the midst of all this scenic splendor."[4]

In keeping with this theme of escape, not only the homes but also the lives of the Arroyo Blanco residents are more completely removed from the city than those of their counterparts in Camptown. Delaney writes for a nature magazine from his home computer; his wife sells real estate in nearby communities—to other families who are also seeking to escape the racial and ethnic diversity of the city.

In the 1960s and 1970s, social scientists criticized earlier views of suburbanization for oversimplifying the suburban experience and overestimating the impact of suburban living. In the 1980s and 1990s, when arguments about the political importance of the suburbs again gained popular currency, social scientists seemed to assume that the same criticisms that had been voiced several decades earlier were still valid, and that contemporary representations of suburbia were as much myth as those of the 1950s. As a consequence, they also failed to take note of the elements of the contemporary suburban myths that make them new—and that give them potentially important political implications.

While political commentators and reporters have not hesitated to argue that understanding the suburbs is central to understanding contemporary politics, political science has largely ignored the relationship between modern suburbs and political behavior. And social scientists who do argue that the suburbs are politically important do not attempt to account for the fact that the same conclusion was rejected by political scientists in the 1960s and 1970s. To address this gap, this book explores both historical and contemporary suburban political behavior. Analyses of census data, public opinion, congressional behavior, and party platforms are used to demonstrate how the connection between suburban living and political behavior has changed over time—and emerged in recent years as a significant feature of the political landscape.

The rise of a distinctive suburban politics is a relatively recent occurrence. National survey data from the 1950s to the 1990s reveal that only since the 1980s has a clear and consistent relationship developed between living in a suburb and distinctive political attitudes and behaviors. Two factors have fostered the recent emergence of a distinctive suburban politics that transcends socioeconomic characteristics: the increase in urban problems, and the evolution of suburbs into self-contained communities.

In this volume, regression analysis is used to demonstrate that city and suburban dwellers do think differently about national politics and vote differently in presidential and congressional elections. Combining census data with national survey data offers evidence that these initial differences narrow when the suburban area in which a respondent lives experiences citylike problems, and increase when the racial and economic differences between the suburban area and its nearby city increase.

One of the implications of these distinctive suburban attitudes is that party competition is premised, in part, on a vision of voters who live in particular kinds of locations. An analysis of congressional representation shows that as congressional districts become increasingly suburban, they are more likely to be represented by a Republican member of Congress, and their representatives are less likely to have a liberal voting record, even after other district characteristics are taken into account.

These findings have two important, but potentially contradictory, implications for urban policymaking, which will be discussed in more detail in the final chapter of the book. First, as older suburbs come to experience some of the problems usually associated with cities, the possibility of city-suburb coalitions in support of federal programs increases. Second, to the extent that cities and suburbs within the same metropolitan area continue to be home to very different populations, suburban residents are likely to continue to withdraw their support for federal spending and increase their support for the political party that favors devolution of power to the state and local levels. Therefore, if suburban decline is accompanied by even more severe decline in neighboring cities, suburban dwellers may have little interest in forming city-suburb coalitions.

Notes

1. "Camptown" and "Arroyo Blanco" are fictional place names taken from two novels that seem to embody the suburban myths of their time: Charles Mergendahl's novel *It's Only Temporary* (New York: Doubleday, 1950) and T. Coraghessan Boyle's novel *The Tortilla Curtain* (New York: Penguin Books, 1995). Mergendahl's Camptown bears more than a passing resemblance to the real suburban community of Levittown. Boyle's Arroyo Blanco is modeled on the gated communities of Los Angeles after the 1992 riots.

2. Mergendahl, *It's Only Temporary,* 9.

3. Boyle, *Tortilla Curtain*, 30.

4. Ibid., 39.

CHAPTER TWO

Political Science and the Suburbs

Indeed, the propensity to speak of a "suburban vote" may be a meaningless extension of the "place theory" implied in speaking of a "rural vote" or "urban vote." The political relevance of the two latter terms is not based simply on the fact that one group lives in the city whereas the other lives in the country; the rural-urban distinction is a social-economic-cultural distinction, and without any doubt suburban tracts are typically urban culturally.

Bennett M. Berger, *Working-Class Suburb*

This year will see the first presidential election in which a majority of the voters will in all likelihood be suburbanites—the first election of the suburban century. . . . Can suburban voters, then, be said to have a defining characteristic? Yes. . . .

William Schneider, "The Suburban Century Begins: The Real Meaning of the 1992 Election"

From "angry white males" to "soccer moms," talk of the suburban voter has dominated much of the news reporting and political commentary of the last several election cycles. The proportion of the United States population living in suburbs—as opposed to rural or urban areas—had grown from one-quarter of the population in 1950 to one-third by 1960; by 1990 almost half of Americans lived in suburbs.[1] Many contemporary observers of American politics argue that this population shift, like the earlier shift from rural to urban areas, has important consequences for American politics.

The distinctiveness of suburban voters now looms large in popular analyses of American politics. In the 1996 presidential campaign, for example, a number of political observers referred to candidate Bob Dole's need to attract the "suburban soccer mom" vote.[2] But while this focus on the suburban woman was peculiar to 1996, the focus on the suburban voter in general is not. During the 1992 presidential election, commentator William Schneider declared in the *Atlantic Monthly* that the era of the suburban voter had arrived and that the Democrats needed to pursue a "suburban strategy if they intended to win."[3] Schneider was not alone in attributing great importance to the fact that 1992 marked the first election in which a majority of the votes would be cast by suburbanites: articles in the *New York Times, The Economist,* and *Congressional Quarterly Weekly Report* all made similar claims.[4]

Two years later, reports of the congressional elections were filled with descriptions of angry white males—presumed suburban dwellers—and their significant role in the Republican sweep of Congress. In the aftermath of the election, the *New York Times* entertainment section even carried a front-page feature declaring that "the theme of both the new Congress and mid-1990s rock is the same: Revenge of the 'Burbs.'"[5]

Given that suburbanization seems to play a central role in much contemporary political analysis, one might expect political scientists to have devoted significant attention to the topic. But this is not the case. Although suburbanization received attention from academics during the 1950s and 1960s, relatively little recent work has been done in the area—in part because the earlier studies were able to uncover little evidence that suburbanization had an independent political effect. Perhaps as a consequence, the literature on the political consequences of contemporary suburbanization tends to take the form of "thought pieces" rather than hard empirical analysis.

One field of study within political science does, however, take a more empirical approach to the subject of location by emphasizing the role of context in political behavior.[6] While this work on contextual effects does not deal explicitly with suburbanization, it does raise the possibility that the type of community or environment in which people reside affects political behavior independently of individual socioeconomic characteristics. In other words, an exploration of context may reveal that "interdependent electorates, rather than individual voters, shape the course of democratic politics."[7] For example, in *Political Change in Britain*, Butler and Stokes found that the local political environment had a significant impact on party support. In resort towns that were predominantly Conservative, the Conservative Party captured more of the working-class vote; in mining towns that were predominantly Labour, Labour captured a high proportion of the middle- class vote.[8] In more recent studies of American politics, a number of researchers have argued that context—primarily because it determines to whom people talk—has a significant independent effect on vote choice and racial attitudes.[9]

The goal of this book is to provide a statistical analysis of contemporary suburban voting behavior and political attitudes. The premise is that in order to understand suburban voters, it is necessary not only to understand their individual-level socioeconomic characteristics but also the environment—both the suburb itself and the wider metropolitan area—in which the voters live.

People in different kinds of localities think differently about national politics. In much the same way that Key argued that a contextual variable—the size of the black population—affects political behavior by changing the calculus involved in the decision to vote, this book shows how living in a suburb affects vote choice and policy preferences by altering the decision-making calculus.[10] This effect is particularly strong in the United States today—where, as political scientist Margaret Weir has argued, local autonomy and distinctive features of U.S. social policy have "made the costs and benefits of living in one political jurisdiction over another substantial."[11]

This chapter sets the stage for the empirical analysis with a brief survey of earlier research on the suburbs and a detailed examination of contemporary arguments about suburbia. The concluding section of the chapter offers a number of reasons to believe in the recent emergence of a distinctive suburban politics despite the fact that one did not exist during the 1960s and early 1970s.

The Emergence of Suburbia

Our property seems to me the most beautiful in the world. It is so close to Babylon that we enjoy all the advantages of the city, and yet when we come home we are away from all the noise and dust.[12]

Despite the relatively recent onslaught of popular analyses of suburbia, the seeds of the "suburban century" were sown long ago. Within the United States, histories of suburbanization usually place the emergence of a recognizable suburban pattern in the nineteenth century. For example, Kenneth T. Jackson writes in *Crabgrass Frontier: The Suburbanization of the United States* that while "in 1840 suburbs had not yet developed into a recognizable entity, . . . by 1890, . . . only a half a century later, the suburban image was quite distinct from that of large cities."[13] In *Streetcar Suburbs*, Sam Bass Warner shows that in the Boston area, the change in the form of the metropolis that had occurred by the end of the nineteenth century was made possible by the invention of alternative means of travel that made locations farther removed from the city center viable places to live.[14]

In the 1930s, 1940s, and continuing into the 1970s, the movement to outlying areas was reinforced by federal housing policies and mortgage guarantee programs that encouraged people to buy homes in the suburbs and perpetuated segregated settlement patterns. Innovations in transportation again became important in the 1950s, when the large amounts of federal monies that were poured into the construction of a major highway system made communities even farther from city centers accessible to commuters.

The Suburban Myths

A car moved down the street. It was loaded with men about his own age. . . . It stopped at the Silers' house, where a man got out, waved, and walked up the steps. The door opened and the pregnant woman kissed him. The car moved on and stopped at the next house. A man went to the door and a woman kissed him. It was like that all the way down the street until the car turned the corner and disappeared in the dusk.[15]

As the number of people living in suburbs continued to increase, the 1950s saw the emergence of a set of suburban myths. Suburbanization was described as signaling the loss of community, and the prevalent image of the suburbanite was that of an atomized individual without ties to his neighbors.[16] But almost as quickly as these myths arose, sociologists began to debunk them: during the 1960s, for example, researchers argued for a less negative depiction of the suburbs, observing that they were home not only to the white middle class but also to a much more representative cross-section of Americans.[17] Sociologists found no evidence that suburban residents were any less likely than city dwellers to have contacts with neighbors and community groups.

Between the mid-1960s and the early 1970s, while sociologists turned their attention to the myths of suburban culture, political scientists focused on some of the myths attached to suburban political life. Much of the work dealt with what was fast becoming conventional wisdom: the idea that the move to the suburbs either caused or was indicative of increased support for the Republican Party. As more Americans moved to the suburbs, so the argument went, the Republican Party would come to dominate American politics. Political scientists, however, found little evidence to support this claim, concluding instead that individual characteristics, such as race and income, rather than locale, determined political behavior.

For example, Zikmund analyzed suburban voting in presidential elections from 1948 to 1964 and found that suburban voting in general followed the national trends for each election. He also found that despite huge increases in population size, the political composition of most suburbs remained stable: as a Republican suburb grew in population, it remained Republican. But Zikmund argued that this was evidence not of conversion to the new political environment but of people's tendency to move to suburbs where similar people already lived: a Republican is more likely to move to a Republican suburb.[18] In another article, Zikmund noted that the responses of suburbanites and urbanites to questions on political attitudes did not differ significantly and that the largest differences were intermetropolitan rather than intrametropolitan.[19] Similarly, Wirt et al. found that "apparent city-suburb differences in partisan political attitudes are primarily attributable to demographic differences between the two locales"; and, in their discussion of suburban political behavior, Greer and Greer held that "the key variables seem to be socioeconomic status, ethnicity (including religion), and life style."[20]

How can the findings of earlier researchers be reconciled with current views of the political significance of suburbanization? First, the claims of suburban dominance in American politics to which these early studies responded were perhaps overblown. The expectation of massive conversion to the Republican Party among suburbanites ignored the strong relationship between socioeconomic characteristics and political support. And the assumption that the Democratic Party would fail to adapt to changing demographics—and simply allow the Republicans to dominate—was equally unrealistic. Given these considerations, it is perhaps not surprising that analyses of suburban voting patterns in the 1960s and 1970s revealed little support for claims of a distinctive suburban political behavior.

But what of today's conventional wisdom about the politics of suburbanites: Is the contemporary view of suburbia as much myth as that which developed in the 1950s? If a distinct suburban political behavior did not exist in the past, why should it be expected today? There are three possible reasons that a new exploration of suburbanization might uncover significant political consequences. First, earlier studies—which were often focused simply on presidential vote or party identification—may not have correctly identified the "effect" (that is, the dependent variable) that suburbanization was supposed to influence. Although contemporary discussions of suburban politics do suggest that the Republican Party maintains an advantage in the suburbs, the arguments are more complex than the simple claim that suburbanites are more likely to vote Republican. By adding a wider range of dependent variables, the analysis in this volume may help to reveal previously unnoticed effects.

The second possible explanation is simply that twenty years have passed since the last time this issue was given serious attention: suburbanization is now more pervasive than ever, and presidents and policies have changed. Third, quantitative methodology is more sophisticated than it was when the earlier analyses were performed. Much of the work involved correlations or simply reported percentages. This third possible explanation must be explored in order to rule out the possibility that a suburban politics did exist previously but was overlooked by researchers at the time.

Contemporary Views of Suburbia

He made his way through the familiar streets, the Vias and Calles and Avenidas of this, his exclusive private community in the hills, composed entirely of Spanish Mission-style homes with orange tile roofs, where the children grew into bigots, the incomes swelled and the property values rose disproportionately.[21]

Current discussions of suburbia generally take one of two perspectives. The first category of work takes an institutional approach, analyzing the development of suburbia in relation to the national and local government actions that permitted, encouraged, and shaped the growth of the suburbs. In the second category are the less empirical, more descriptive discussions of what the growth of a suburban electorate means for American politics.

Research undertaken from an institutional perspective provides important insight into the forces behind the formation of suburbia as we see it today, but the effect of suburban living on political behavior is discussed only in passing. In *Cities by Contract: The Politics of Municipal Incorporation*, Gary Miller describes how, in Los Angeles, institutional factors ease the way for incorporation—which, in turn, allows wealthy, largely white suburbs to separate from the poorer parts of the county and keep their resources for themselves.[22] Similarly, Michael Danielson argues in *The Politics of Exclusion* that local control of zoning ordinances and the federal government's responsiveness to local interests have permitted the development and extension of settlement patterns in which residents are segregated by race and income.[23]

Implicit in these arguments is the assumption that in these newly created jurisdictions, residents' sense of connectedness or responsibility to a community extends only to the closest boundary. However, Miller and Danielson are less concerned with this attitude and its implications for national politics than with the way in which government policies have allowed the "localist" perspective to be institutionalized with the formation of local government boundaries. So, for example, Danielson blames institutional support for segregated suburbs on the responsiveness of the federal government to white middle-class interests.[24] However, to take this argument one step further, the very availability of these suburbs as refuges from urban problems further shapes these middle-class interests and ensures that they continue to be distinguishable from those of the poor and working class.

A related set of literature, which focuses on the politics of growth within suburbs, illustrates the ways in which suburban growth patterns reflect the preferences of suburban residents—and in which land-use policies have been used to maintain the exclusive nature of suburban communities.[25] While this research does account for the successful translation of suburban policy preferences into policy outcomes, it remains focused on the local rather than national level, and it fails to account for the emergence of these distinctive suburban political preferences.

Contemporary examinations of the political behavior of suburbanites do not offer the same cultural critique that was made during the 1950s. Instead of depicting suburbia as the home of status-conscious automatons, the newer descriptions emphasize the suburb's role as a refuge, a place where people attempt to insulate themselves from the problems of "others." Earlier studies of suburbia were interested in demonstrating that suburbanites lacked a sense of community. Contemporary discussions turn this argument on its head, arguing that suburbanites' identification with and allegiance to their local suburb can have pernicious effects at the national level. The literature that makes this argument can be divided into works that are design oriented and works that are explicitly political.

Contemporary critiques of suburbia offered from the perspective of urban planning or design are more than denouncements of the blandness of tract housing. Books like Philip Langdon's *A Better Place to Live: Reshaping the American Suburb,* and Mike Davis's *City of Quartz* draw connections between suburban design, the privatization of space, and the politics of place.[26] Langdon describes developers' deliberate efforts to appeal to only one segment of the population with any one housing development, thus ensuring that buyers will find neighbors of the same age and economic status. "Today," he argues, this "tendency is pushed to an unprecedented extreme by marketers and developers who play not only on people's positive yearnings for like-minded neighbors but also on their fears." He quotes a marketing executive: "When you work for developers, you learn that almost everything that goes on in development is based on fear and flight.... It's based on fear of cities, fear of the people that are in cities, and flight from them."[27] Ultimately, Langdon argues, local settlement patterns have costly national effects:

> The costs of a deliberately segregated pattern of development weigh on society as a whole. Barriers between one residential area and another foster a breakdown of the larger community. It becomes harder to create towns, cities and metropolitan areas that pull together, focusing on common interests and shared goals.

Energy that could be channeled into the betterment of the society
is dissipated by the growth of an "us against them" mentality.[28]

In his history of Los Angeles, Davis makes the same argument as
Miller about the way in which incorporation and zoning have enabled
suburban enclaves to rally "around the defense of household equity
and residential privilege."[29] In addition, he points to the pervasiveness
of design features that also reflect, in an even starker way, the desire
of suburbanites to insulate themselves from the problems of the outside world. Davis describes "a rhetoric of social welfare that calculates
the interests of the urban poor and the middle classes as a zero-sum
game. In cities like Los Angeles . . . one observes an unprecedented
tendency to merge urban design, architecture and the police appara-
tus into a single, comprehensive security effort."[30] One effect is that
public spaces increasingly disappear or are made inhospitable. Another is that "new luxury developments outside the city limits have
often become fortress cities, complete with encompassing walls, restricted entry points with guard posts, overlapping private and public
police services, and even privatized roadways."[31] Finally, Davis describes how Los Angeles suburbs have succeeded in recasting political
debate to reflect their own concerns: "The appalling destruction and
misery within Los Angeles' inner city areas became the great non-
issue during the 1980s, while the impact of growth upon affluent
neighborhoods occupied center-stage."[32]

This urban planning and design literature offers important in-
sights into the design features that characterize much of suburbia—and into the ways in which design shapes not only the aesthetic
but the social environment. How architecture and design are related
to politics is less clearly defined. The suggestion is that particular
housing patterns shape residents' social landscapes, largely by determining with whom they interact. This in turn shapes the political
agenda by influencing which issues people see as important. While
provocative, this argument relies more on the authors' impressions
than on systematic analysis of the relationship between location and
political behavior. In addition, while urban planning and design literature does a good job of describing suburban design features that can
be expected to produce particular political outcomes, it does not
address to what extent these features are common to all suburbs,
some suburbs, or only a very few suburbs. This is an important omis-
sion because much of the new literature dealing with the suburbs

argues that the term describes such a broad array of communities as to have lost a great deal of its meaning.

The more explicitly political literature addressing contemporary suburbanization intersects with the urban planning and design literature in interesting ways but also ultimately fails to offer more than nonsystematic observations as evidence of a distinctive suburban politics. Although the authors who take a political approach are much less careful than those in urban planning and design to specify exactly which features of suburbia generate the expected political effects, they are even more specific about the nature of those effects: a turning away from national problems and national remedies and a turning toward the local community.

An eloquent rendition of this argument can be found in Edsall and Edsall's account of why the Democratic Party can no longer elect a president.[33] In a book written before Clinton's 1992 victory, the Edsalls argued that the Republicans had successfully divided the Democratic coalition by focusing on the issues of race and taxes. The suburbs were fundamental to this strategy because "the accelerated growth of suburbs has made it possible for many Americans to fulfill a basic drive toward civic participation—involvement in schools, cooperation in community endeavors, a willingness to support and to pay for public services—within a smaller universe, separate and apart from the consuming failure, crime, welfarism, decay—and blackness—of the older cities."[34] In turn, Edsall and Edsall conclude, "with a majority of the electorate equipped to address its own needs through local government, not only will urban blacks become increasingly isolated by city-county boundaries, but support for the federal government, a primary driving force behind black advancement, is likely to diminish."[35] Here is the argument that is missing from the institutional literature: the preferences of white middle-class people allowed the development of segregated suburbs to continue unabated; in turn, the existence of these suburbs further shaped these preferences, diminishing support for the federal government.

The work of former secretary of labor Robert B. Reich offers a similar argument: in Reich's view, the emphasis on localism that began during the Reagan era is a dangerous trend, given that communities tend to be segregated along income lines.

By the 1980s the meaning of neighborhood had changed. What had once been small towns or ethnic sections within larger cities had given way to economic enclaves whose members had little in common with one another but their average incomes.

The idea of neighborhood benevolence—of neighbors looking after one another—had little practical meaning in this new context.... The idea of community as neighborhood offered a way of enjoying the sentiment of benevolence without the burden of acting on it. Since responsibility ended at the borders of one's neighborhood, and most Americans could rest assured that their neighbors were not in dire straits, the apparent requirements of charity could be exhausted at small cost. If the inhabitants of another neighborhood needed help, they should look to one another; let them solve their problems, and we'll solve our own.[36]

Reich is pointing to the way in which the very existence of the suburbs allows the formation of distinctive attitudes and ideas. Support for the principle of neighbors helping neighbors—rather than for the principle of the federal government helping neighbors—is more attractive to voters whose neighbors are middle class than to those whose neighbors are poor or working class.

As a final, influential example of this line of argument, political commentator William Schneider notes that the growth of the suburbs poses serious problems for the Democratic Party because suburbanites are not supportive of activist government, preferring to pay for the private—and therefore targeted—provision of services within the suburban environment. Schneider writes that the suburban reply to the question "Isn't it in the national interest to bail out the cities?" has been to create walled communities, and he describes the choice to live in the suburbs as the choice of the private over the public: private space, private entertainment, private government.[37] Again, this is a choice that is viable precisely because income-segregated suburbs exist.

Why Now?

If the new perspectives on the suburbs focus less on conformity and support for a particular party and more on the idea of a retreat in defense of local boundaries, then the search for relevant trends in the past twenty years must explain what made this "defensive localism" both possible and desirable.[38]

The Possibility

For the rest of his days he'd have to feel like a criminal driving into his own community, excusing himself to some jerk in a crypto-fascist uniform, making special arrangements every time a friend visited or a package needed to be delivered. He thought of the development he'd grown up in, the fenceless expanse of lawns, the shared space, the deep lush marshy woods where he'd first discovered ferns, frogs, garter snakes, the whole shining envelope of creation. There was nothing like that anymore. Now there were fences. Now there were gates.[39]

In the attempt to debunk the suburban myths of the 1950s, one of the earliest arguments made was that the suburbs were much more diverse than the myths allowed. Support for this perspective would seem only to have increased in the past few decades. First, it is not only middle-class whites who live in suburbs: increasingly, suburbs have become home to African Americans and lower-income residents as well.[40] Second, suburbs are no longer just bedroom communities: indeed, Joel Garreau and Robert Fishman, in separate works, have both made convincing arguments that many of today's suburbs are actually new forms of cities—self-contained entities complete with business parks, shopping centers, and entertainment complexes.[41] In *Edge City: Life on the New Frontier,* Garreau claims that these agglomerations of housing and commerce are the new city, and that it is only because they are so different from what we have previously thought of as a city that we have failed to see them for what they are. In *Bourgeois Utopias: The Rise and Fall of Suburbia*, Fishman makes a similar argument: because, with the rise of "technoburbs," the suburbs no longer need the city, the suburban era has been brought to an end.[42]

While both Garreau and Fishman certainly make a persuasive case that suburbs are no longer simply bedroom communities, it is not clear what this ultimately means for debate about the suburbanization of politics. It may be that this very diversification of functions within the suburb has made possible the rise of a distinctly suburban politics. Fishman himself offers support for this idea when he observes that the beginning of suburbanization was actually a period of strength for cities because the suburbs were dependent on the city for employment, shopping, and entertainment. With the emergence of technoburbs, however, residents have access to all the functions of the city without ever having to leave the suburb.

Despite Fishman's enthusiastic description of this new city form, with its potential to fulfill its residents' "basic hopes for comfortable homes in sylvan settings with easy access to good schools, good jobs, and recreational facilities,"[43] Fishman does acknowledge one important distinction between the old and the new form of city:

> Unfortunately, residents of the new city have generally resisted attempts to build low-income housing in middle-class areas and have discouraged public transportation links. They want to keep the new city's expanding tax base for themselves and to avoid any direct fiscal responsibility for the urban poor. The new city has thus walled itself off from the problems of the inner city in a way that the Social Darwinists of the 19th Century could only envy.[44]

The existence of "new cities," with many of the amenities of the old city and few of its social problems, makes it increasingly possible for today's suburbanites to live without giving a thought to the city and its residents. The very fact that suburbanites never visit the city—and, in their day-to-day suburban lives, are seemingly unaffected by its problems—permits the development of distinctive suburban attitudes toward national government and allows suburban dwellers to push the needs of the poor and the working class out of their minds. Carl Abbott makes this point in his discussion of Sun Belt cities: "When most residents of the [suburb] have no contact, no concern, and no interest in the old core neighborhoods, suburbanites will tend to direct their political life without particular reference to the central city."[45]

While edge cities may not correspond to earlier images of suburbia, they make even easier the development of enclaves where residents can insulate themselves from the problems of older cities. Residents of the earlier bedroom suburbs had contact with the city when they went to their jobs in downtown office buildings, when they went shopping, and when they wanted a night out at the theater. Residents of edge cities can work, shop, and enjoy a night out without ever entering the city. A *Business Week* article on the role of suburbanites in the 1992 election makes a similar point: "For decades, urban planners believed that a metropolitan area's economic health depended on the vitality of the urban core. But today the suburb is no longer sub to the urb. Outlying communities, with their megamalls and office parks, are becoming economically self-sufficient. Many suburban residents rarely venture into the city, either to work or to play."[46]

The attitude that this shift is likely to engender was summed up by a resident of Boston's suburbs. When asked by the *Boston Globe* about the approaching mayoral election in Boston, he replied, "Boston's problems are horrendous, with the shootings, the schools. But we're in our own little world. My little world is Needham tax bills, the water rates, capping the local dump. I can't get too worked up about Boston's mayoral race."[47] Also describing the increasing lack of connection between city and suburb, Jackson points out that while earlier suburbs were often named after the city they surrounded—for example, North or West Chicago—they are now given names that invoke rural, bucolic images—Park Forest, Highland Hills, River Grove.[48]

Further evidence along the same lines can be found in the results of a November 1991 poll of New York area residents conducted for the *New York Times*.[49] The poll found that suburban residents do indeed have fewer reasons to go to the city than before. Of chief wage earners in the suburbs, only 22 percent worked in the city, while 58 percent worked in their home county. As for leisure, 51 percent of suburbanites said that they spend an evening or day in the city less frequently than they did five years ago. As might be expected, with this diminishing contact seems to have come a diminished feeling of connection: 51 percent of suburban residents said that "events in the city have hardly any impact on their lives today"—an increase from the 39 percent who responded this way in a 1978 survey.

If, as Reich argues, "the idea of community as neighborhood offer[s] a way of enjoying the sentiment of benevolence without the burden of acting on it,"[50] then it becomes even easier to maintain this sense of benevolence if the needs of people in other communities are completely invisible. The changes in the function of suburbs—no longer primarily residential, they are now also places for work and recreation—have led some observers to question the validity of talking about suburbs as distinct entities. But it is these very changes that allow today's suburbanites to live their lives insulated from the needs of cities and their residents—and that may have been, then, a necessary ingredient in the emergence of a distinct suburban politics. As noted earlier, Schneider believes that suburbanites have answered the question of whether the suburbs need a vital urban core by building walled communities.[51] It might also be said that suburbanites have given their answer by building business parks, hotels, and entertainment centers right alongside their homes.

Although it has received less attention than other changes in the suburban landscape, the privatization of services is another trend that helps suburbanites to lead lives independent of the city. Edsall and Edsall have argued that suburbanization has generally allowed whites to satisfy a desire for services in a way that guarantees "the highest possible return to themselves on their tax dollars."[52] By ensuring that only those who directly contribute receive the service, privatization helps guarantee that residents' money is used to pay for services that only they will enjoy. And by furthering the view that services are something that local communities provide only for themselves, privatization enables suburban dwellers to concentrate on their own community's needs.

In *Privatopia: Homeowner Associations and the Rise of Residential Private Government*, Evan McKenzie describes this process at work in the development and expansion of common-interest housing developments, which operate almost like private cities with private governments.[53] McKenzie observes that because such developments finance the private provision of services through annual dues from residents, residents inevitably come to resent paying taxes for publicly provided services that they no longer need. This situation has had concrete political consequences at both the state and national levels because associations representing common-interest developments (CIDs) have argued that CID residents—who must pay both property taxes and homeowner association assessments—are unfairly subjected to double taxation.[54]

McKenzie's description of the consequences of CID housing provides concrete evidence for Schneider's contention that the move to the suburb is the choice of the private over the public. While CID housing existed during the 1960s, when the political implications of suburban living were first being discussed, the growth of CID housing exploded during the following decades: while "there were fewer than five hundred such homeowner associations in 1964 . . . by 1992, there were 150,000 associations privately governing an estimated 32 million Americans. . . . [and] constituting more than 11 percent of American housing."[55] One in eight Americans now lives under the jurisdiction of a homeowner's association.[56] Moreover, citing a survey by the

Advisory Commission on Intergovernmental Relations (ACIR), McKenzie finds that

> CIDs have become so much the norm for new housing that, as the ACIR notes, "In many rapidly developing areas, such as those in California, nearly all new residential development is within the jurisdiction of residential community associations." As CIDs spread, and as old housing is replaced by new CID housing, consumer choice is increasingly restricted. In short, growing numbers of Americans who wish to purchase new houses are going to be living in CIDs, and under the rule of private governments, regardless of their preferences.[57]

CID housing is not simply becoming an increasingly common form of housing, it is becoming particularly common in areas where new housing is being built—that is, in the suburbs.[58]

Developments in suburban organization and governance—such as privatization and CIDs—helped lay the groundwork for a distinctive suburban politics because they meant that residents no longer had to see the signs of the poverty that is concentrated in urban areas. Being thus protected from the signs of poverty made it easier to focus inward on the local community. Another factor that strengthened this inward focus was the redefinition, in the early 1980s, of the needs of the urban poor as illegitimate. Conservatives such as Charles Murray and Lawrence Mead argued that it was precisely the costly national social programs of the earlier decades that had perpetuated poverty and socially undesirable behavior in urban areas.[59] The poor had not only failed to help themselves, they had adopted ever more irresponsible behaviors because social programs both permitted and encouraged them to do so. By making it acceptable to oppose the provision of social services, this conservative critique of the welfare state permitted people to withdraw support from programs that were aimed at providing a national solution to the problems of poverty without feeling that they were being uncaring. This redefinition of the problems of the urban poor, combined with the fact that residents of self-contained suburban communities very rarely came into contact with urban poverty, increased the acceptability of an ideology of localism. The fact that this ideology inevitably left poor communities without the resources to help their residents could be conveniently forgotten—or justified as the result of irresponsible behavior on the part of the poor.

The Desire

"I'd like to open my arms to everybody in the world, no matter how poor they are or what country they come from . . . but you know as well as I do that those days are past." He shook his head sadly. "L.A. stinks. The world stinks. Why kid ourselves? That's why we're here, that's why we got out. You want to save the world, go to Calcutta and sign on with Mother Teresa. I say that gate is as necessary, as vital, essential and un-do-withoutable as the roofs over our heads and the dead bolts on our doors. Face up to it," he rumbled.[60]

Two important economic trends that combined during the 1970s and 1980s may also help to explain why a distinct suburban politics may have emerged during this time period rather than before. The first was the widespread urban crisis that affected most major central cities during the 1970s.[61] Summing up the condition of many cities during those years, Bradbury, Downs, and Small describe the population loss that ranged from moderate to high, often with severe consequences:

These declines have caused serious fiscal and other problems. The near bankruptcy of New York City in 1975, and the subsequent default by Cleveland in 1978, dramatized a "fiscal squeeze" that has also forced other cities to cut service levels or capital-facility maintenance. . . . Moreover, many cities contain decaying neighborhoods occupied mainly by poor households and devastated by housing abandonment, arson, vandalism, and high crime rates.[62]

In part because of earlier waves of suburbanization and in part because of national economic forces, cities in the 1970s became even less desirable as places to live for those who had other options. While the United States has never been a nation enamored of urban areas, the cities in this decade came increasingly to embody, in the minds of the middle class, all that was bad. A *New York Times* poll of the New York region found that four in ten suburban residents described their image of the city as a bad one: one interviewee commented, for example, that when she thought of the city she thought of "the Utah tourist who came to see the United States Open tennis tournament and lost his life in a New York subway."[63] Even among city dwellers, a 1991 *Newsweek* poll found that 87 percent would have preferred to be living elsewhere.[64] At the same time, then, as the suburbanites' ability to ignore the city increased, the desire to avoid it—and the more and more troubled picture it presented—also increased.

This shift might not necessarily have led suburban dwellers to embrace an ideology of localism and to abandon the idea of national solutions to problems if it had not coincided with other events. As a consequence of the same national economic forces that were hurting the cities, the national government became increasingly unable and unwilling to pay for expensive social programs—particularly when most of the constituents of national politicians resided in areas that were not the main beneficiaries of these programs. Normative beliefs about the benefits of decentralized government coincided with a number of new economic realities—in particular, the rise of the federal deficit—in a way that altered the relationship between the federal government and cities. Devolution of responsibility to lower levels of government was an explicit element of Ronald Reagan's ideology as presented in his 1980 inaugural address; at the same time, the rise of the federal deficit fundamentally changed perceptions of the federal government's ability to fund urban programs.

A related issue—and one that is perhaps most relevant for the recent emergence of a distinctive suburban vote—is that middle-class suburban dwellers in the 1980s began to feel economically insecure. Newman, among others, has explored the ways in which a new generation of suburban dwellers have found themselves increasingly unable to maintain the same standard of living as their parents.[65] Homeownership, leisure time, and savings are increasingly hard to attain, and a good education and a job with a reputable company no longer ensure lifetime employment. It makes sense that as suburbanites feel increasingly insecure themselves, they are less likely to feel able or willing to support programs for others that are paid for with their own tax dollars.

The fencing-off of a community is not only a rejection of what lies outside but also a fear of losing what lies inside. The fence both keeps the bad out (in this instance, groups in need of expensive social services) and keeps the good in (in this instance, individuals with taxable income and relatively few social-service needs). This mindset is vividly depicted by Danielson when he describes the arrival in suburbia of some urbanlike problems:

> The growth of crime, racial conflict, drug abuse, neighborhood decay, and other "city" problems in suburbia have not noticeably stimulated suburban concern with urban interdependence or the need for cooperative ventures with the central city. Quite the opposite has occurred in many instances. As social problems become more serious in the suburbs, suburban determination is reinforced to build the walls of political and social separation even higher in order to keep out a plague whose source is seen as the city and its lower-income and black residents.[66]

The more fearful suburban residents are that they will be brought face-to-face with the same problems that they associate with the city, the more they desire to separate from the city.

This desire to separate from the city as a response to urban ills is starkly illustrated by the incorporation campaigns of some communities. Wealthier areas of existing cities or counties seek to break away and form their own political unit, which will allow them to control their own local taxes and services.[67] In California during the 1980s, the number of newly incorporating cities was double that of the previous decade. The increasing attractiveness of incorporation in California was attributed to the passage of Proposition 13—which, by limiting property tax increases, allowed local governments to capture control of local property taxes without the risk that the county would raise taxes by a corresponding amount to replace lost revenue. Similarly, the existence of the Lakewood Plan, which allowed cities to contract with the county for services, meant that newly incorporated localities could control local service levels without having to provide the services themselves.[68]

While the desire to separate from cities has been quite evident during the past decade, some observers have argued that with the rise of citylike ills in older suburbs, suburban residents may begin to perceive that they have common interests with city residents. Consequently, they may reject "defensive localism" in favor of the creation of a city-suburb coalition whose goal would be to involve the federal government in solving the problems that cities and suburbs share.[69] (This possibility will be discussed further in chapter 6.)

Before turning to the analysis of political behavior, it is necessary to further investigate the issue of suburban diversity. In the next chapter, census data is used to explore precisely what is meant by the term *suburban*.

Notes

1. William Schneider, "The Suburban Century Begins: The Real Meaning of the 1992 Election," *The Atlantic Monthly,* July 1992, 33–44.

2. See, for example, Carez Goldberg, "Political Battle of the Sexes Is Tougher than Ever; Suburbs' Soccer Moms, Fleeing the G.O.P., Are Much Sought," *New York Times,* 6 October 1996, p. A1; Gina Kolata, "Vying for the Breast Vote," *New York Times,* 6 November 1996, p. D5. Alison Mitchell, "Clinton Campaign Puts an Emphasis on Female Voters," *New York Times,* 28 October 1996, p. A1.

3. Schneider, "Suburban Century."

4. Rhodes Cook, "As Suburban Loyalty Is Tested, Bush Isn't Making the Grade," *Congressional Quarterly Weekly Report,* 26 September 1992; "Suburbia: A Republican Way of Life," *The Economist,* 11 May 1991; "The Suburban Vote Conforming to What?" *The Economist,* 17 October 1992; Robert W. Merry, "Suburbia Ascendant: Dawn of a New Era," *Congressional Quarterly Weekly Report,* 29 June 1992; Robert Reinhold, "Chasing Votes from Big Cities to the Suburbs," *New York Times,* 1 June 1992, p. A1.

5. Jon Pareles, "Newt Age Music," *New York Times,* 15 January 1995, pp. B1, B28.

6. Although assumptions about the ability of locale to affect political attitudes are implicit in many contemporary discussions of suburbs, the literature on contextual effects has not generally dealt explicitly with suburbanization. An exception is the recent interest in the relationship between suburbanization and declining levels of civic engagement. Oliver, for example, finds that participation in local politics varies according to the level of income and degree of economic homogeneity in the community. See "The Effects of Metropolitan Economic Segregation on Local Civic Participation," *American Journal of Political Science,* 43, no. 1 (January 1999):186–212; see also Robert Putnam, "Tuning In, Tuning Out: The Strange Disappearance of Social Capital in America," *PS: Political Science and Politics* 28, no. 4 (December 1995).

7. Robert Huckfeldt and John Sprague, "Citizens, Contexts, and Politics," in *Political Science: The State of the Discipline II*, ed. Ada W. Finifter (Washington, D.C.: American Political Science Association, 1993). See also John W. Books and Charles L. Prysby, *Political Behavior and the Local Context* (New York: Praeger, 1991); Thad A. Brown, *Migration and Politics: The Impact of Population Mobility on American Voting Behavior* (Chapel Hill: University of North Carolina Press, 1988).

8. David Butler and Donald Stokes, *Political Change in Britain* (New York: St. Martin's Press, 1969).

9. James M. Glaser, "Back to the Black Belt: Racial Environment and White Racial Attitudes in the South," *Journal of Politics* 56, no. 1 (February 1994); Robert Huckfeldt and John Sprague, "Networks in Context: The Social Flow of Political Information," *American Political Science Review* 81, no. 4 (December 1987); Donald R. Kinder and Tali Mendelberg, "Cracks in American Apartheid: The Political Impact of Prejudice among Desegregated Whites," *Journal of Politics* 57, no. 2 (May 1995); Michael MacKuen and Courtney Brown, "Political Context and Attitude Change," *American Political Science Review* 81, no. 2 (June 1987).

10. See V. O. Key, *Southern Politics in State and Nation* (Knoxville, University of Tennessee Press, 1949). For a poignant account of how where people live can affect their calculation of self-interest—and therefore their politics—see Jonathan Rieder, *The Jews and Italians of Brooklyn against Liberalism* (Cambridge: Harvard University Press, 1985).

11. Margaret Weir, "Poverty, Social Rights, and the Politics of Place in the United States," in *European Social Policy: Between Fragmentation and Integration*, ed. Stephen Leibfried and Paul Pierson (Washington, D.C.: Brookings Institution Press, 1995), 352.

12. From a letter to the King of Persia, written on a clay tablet and dating from 539 B.C.; quoted in Kenneth T. Jackson, *Crabgrass Frontier: The Suburbanization of the United States* (Oxford: Oxford University Press, 1985), 12.

13. Ibid., 45–46. See also Robert Fishman, *Bourgeois Utopias: The Rise and Fall of Suburbia* (New York: Basic Books, 1987).

14. Sam Bass Warner, *Streetcar Suburbs: The Process of Growth in Boston, 1870–1900* (Cambridge: Harvard University Press, 1962).

15. Charles Mergendahl, *It's Only Temporary* (New York: Doubleday, 1950), 17.

16. The classic rendition of this argument can be found in William H. Whyte Jr., *The Organization Man* (New York: Simon and Schuster, 1956).

17. See, for example, Herbert J. Gans, *The Levittowners* (New York: Pantheon Books, 1967); Bennet M. Berger, *Working-Class Suburb* (Berkeley and Los Angeles: University of California Press, 1960).

18. Joseph Zikmund II, "Suburban Voting in Presidential Elections," *Midwest Journal of Political Science* 12, no. 2 (May 1968). Herbert Hirsch also found that suburban voting followed national trends; see "Suburban Voting and National Trends: A Research Note," *Western Political Quarterly* 21, no. 3 (September 1968).

19. Joseph Zikmund II, "A Comparison of Political Attitude and Activity Patterns in Central Cities and Suburbs," *Public Opinion Quarterly* 31, no. 1 (spring 1967).

20. Frederick M. Wirt et al., *On the City's Rim: Politics and Policy in Suburbia* (Lexington, Mass.: D.C. Heath, 1972), 114; Ann Lennarson Greer and Scott Greer, "Suburban Political Behavior: A Matter of Trust," in *The Changing Face of the Suburbs*, ed. Barry Schwartz (Chicago: University of Chicago Press, 1976), 205.

21. T. Coraghessan Boyle, *The Tortilla Curtain* (New York: Penguin Books, 1995), 225.

22. Gary Miller, *Cities by Contract: The Politics of Municipal Incorporation* (Cambridge, Mass: MIT Press, 1981).

23. Michael D. Danielson, *The Politics of Exclusion* (New York: Columbia University Press, 1976).

24. Ibid., 199–242.

25. See, for example, Todd Donovan and Max Neiman, "Citizen Mobilization and the Adoption of Local Growth Control," *Western Political Quarterly* 45, no. 3 (September 1992); Donovan and Neiman, "Community Social Status, Suburban Growth, and Local Government Restrictions on Residential Development," *Urban Affairs Quarterly* 28, no. 2 (December 1992); Arnold Fleischmann and Carol A. Pierannunzi, "Citizens, Development Interests, and Local Land-Use Regulation," *Journal of Politics* 52, no. 3 (August 1990); Mark Schneider, "The Progrowth Entrepreneur in Local Government," *Urban Affairs Review* 29, no. 2 (December 1993).

26. Philip Langdon, *A Better Place to Live: Reshaping the American Suburb* (Amherst: University of Massachusetts Press, 1994); Mike Davis, *City of Quartz: Excavating the Future in Los Angeles* (New York: Vintage Books, 1990).

27. Langdon, *Better Place to Live,* 73.

28. Ibid., 74.

29. Davis, *City of Quartz*, 159.

30. Ibid., 224.

31. Ibid., 244.

32. Ibid., 212.

33. Thomas Byrne Edsall and Mary Edsall, *Chain Reaction: The Impact of Race, Rights, and Taxes on American Politics* (New York: W.W. Norton, 1992).

34. Ibid., 228.

35. Ibid., 231.

36. Robert B. Reich, *Tales of a New America* (New York: Times Books, 1987), 170–71.

37. Schneider, "Suburban Century Begins," 33–44.

38. The term *defensive localism* is used by Weir in "The Politics of Place," 352.

39. Boyle, *Tortilla Curtain*, 42.

40. In fact, social scientists have continued to pay attention to black suburbanization. See, for example, Timothy Bledsoe and Susan Welch, "Residential Context and Racial Solidarity among African Americans," *American Journal of Political Science* 39, no. 2 (May 1995); Mark Schneider and Thomas Phelan, "Black Suburbanization in the 1980s," *Demography* 30, no. 2 (May 1993); John M. Stahura, "Changing Patterns of Suburban Racial Composition, 1970–1980," *Urban Affairs Quarterly* 23, no. 3 (March 1988).

41. Fishman, *Bourgeois Utopias*; Joel Garreau, *Edge City: Life on the New Frontier* (New York: Doubleday, 1991). See also Thomas M. Stanback Jr., *The New Suburbanization: Challenge to the Central City* (Boulder, Colo.: Westview Press, 1991).

42. An important debate about suburbanization deals with city-suburb economic interconnectedness. See, for example, Edward W. Hill, Harold L. Wolman, and Coit Cook Ford III, "Can Suburbs Survive without their Central Cities? Examining the Suburban Dependence Hypothesis," *Urban Affairs Review* 31, no. 2 (November 1995); H. V. Savitch et al., "Ties That Bind: Central Cities, Suburbs, and the New Metropolitan Region," *Economic Development Quarterly* 7, no. 4 (November 1993). However, the question whether economically healthy suburbs require a healthy center city is different from the issue of how much interaction suburban residents have with the central city. As noted later in the book, research maybe able to demonstrate the connection between city and suburban economies, but until suburban residents *experience* this connection, their politics may not reflect this reality.

43. Robert Fishman, "America's New City: Megalopolis Unbound," *Wilson Quarterly* (winter 1990), 30.

44. Ibid., 42.

45. Carl Abbott, *The New Urban America: Growth and Politics in Sunbelt Cities* (Chapel Hill: University of North Carolina Press, 1987), 213.

46. Susan B. Garland, "The Battle of the 'Burbs: Redrawing the Political Map," *Business Week*, 26 November 1990, 80–86.

47. Alan Luppo, "'So What?' Says Suburbia," *Boston Globe*, 10 September 1993, C19.

48. Jackson, *Crabgrass Frontier*, 272.

49. William Glaberson, "For Many in the New York Region, the City Is Ignored and Irrelevant," *New York Times*, 2 January 1992, p. A1; Elizabeth

Kolbert, "Region around New York Sees Ties to City Faltering," *New York Times,* 1 December 1991, p. A1.

50. Reich, *Tales of a New America,* 170–71.

51. Schneider, "Suburban Century Begins," 35.

52. Edsall and Edsall, Chain Reaction, 230–31.

53. Evan McKenzie, *Privatopia: Homeowner Associations and the Rise of Residential Private Government* (New Haven, Conn.: Yale University Press, 1994). See also Edward J. Blakely and Mary Gail Snyder, *Fortress America: Gated Communities in the United States* (Washington, D.C.: Brookings Institution Press; Cambridge, Mass.: Lincoln Institute of Land Policy, 1997).

54. McKenzie, *Privatopia,* 192–97.

55. Ibid., 11.

56. Langdon, *Better Place to Live,* 87.

57. McKenzie, *Privatopia,* 12–13.

58. It should be noted, however, that the proliferation of CIDs is also a trend that allows people to remain in the city and at the same time secede from the problems and costs of the city—as if they had moved to the suburbs. However, until the issue of "double taxation" is decided in favor of CID dwellers, the city at least still benefits from the CID dwellers' tax payments.

59. Charles Murray, *Losing Ground: American Social Policy, 1950–1980* (New York: Basic Books, 1984); Lawrence M. Mead, *Beyond Entitlement: The Social Obligations of Citizenship* (New York: Free Press, 1986).

60. Boyle, *Tortilla Curtain,* 44.

61. For a discussion of the problems that urban areas encountered in the 1970s and 1980s, see Peter Dreier, "America's Urban Crisis: Symptoms, Causes, and Solutions," in *Race, Poverty, and American Cities,* ed. John Charles Boger and Judith Welch Wegner (Chapel Hill: University of North Carolina Press, 1996); John D. Kasarda, "Cities as Places Where People Live and Work: Urban Change and Neighborhood Distress," in *Urban Change in the United States and Western Europe: Comparative Analysis and Policy,* ed. Anita A. Summers, Paul C. Cheshire, and Lanfrenco Senn (Washington, D.C.: Urban Institute Press, 1993).

62. Katherine L. Bradbury, Anthony Downs, and Kenneth A. Small, *Urban Decline and the Future of American Cities* (Washington, D.C.: Brookings Institution Press, 1982), 1–2.

63. Glaberson, "City Ignored and Irrelevant," p. B4.

64. Cited in Renee Loth, "Citifying Suburbia: It Isn't What It Was, US Census Figures Show," *Boston Globe,* 3 November 1991, p. B17.

65. Katherine S. Newman, *Declining Fortunes: The Withering of the American Dream* (New York: Basic Books, 1993).

66. Danielson, *Politics of Exclusion,* 20.

67. B. Drummond Ayres Jr., "Los Angeles, Long Fragmented, Faces Threat of Secession by the San Fernando Valley," *New York Times,* 29 May 1996, p. A10; Nancy Burns, *The Formation of American Local Governments: Private Values in Public Institutions* (New York: Oxford University Press, 1994); Miller, *Cities by Contract.*

68. Miller, *Cities by Contract;* California Assembly Office of Research, *Getting Ahead of the Growth Curve: The Future of Local Government in California* (Sacramento, December 1989).

69. See, for example, Mark Baldassare, *Trouble in Paradise: The Suburban Transformation in America* (New York: Columbia University Press, 1986); Dreier, "America's Urban Crisis;" Louis H. Masotti and Jeffrey K. Hadden, eds., *The Urbanization of the Suburbs* (Beverly Hills: Sage Publications, 1973); Myron Orfield, *Metropolitics: A Regional Agenda for Community and Stability* (Washington, D.C.: Brookings Institution Press; Cambridge, Mass.: Lincoln Institute of Land Policy, 1997).

CHAPTER THREE

What Is a Suburb?

Any study of the national political consequences of suburbanization must deal with two important objections. The first is that the term *suburb* encompasses so many different kinds of localities that its meaning is called into question. The second is that a suburban politics is nothing more than the politics of white middle-class people: it has little to do with location and everything to do with individuals' socio-economic characteristics. This chapter considers both these objections and describes how they will be handled in the subsequent quantitative analysis of public opinion data and congressional data.

In a sense, the two objections are somewhat contradictory. The first says that generalizing about areas labeled "suburban" is futile because such areas are home to many different kinds of popula-tions—white, black, rich, poor—while the second says that it is the similarity of the individuals who live in suburbs that creates the illu-sion of a geographic effect: suburbs are home to a particular kind of politics simply because they are inhabited by people who subscribe to a particular kind of politics; neither the locality itself nor the fact that these individuals are grouped together in one location is important. Despite their seemingly contradictory nature, these two perspectives have both worked as powerful arguments against a renewed discussion of the suburban voter in the 1980s and 1990s.

This chapter explores the first objection by asking the question What is a suburb? Is it possible to generalize about areas we call suburbs, and if so, what is the basis for the generalization? This discussion will, in turn, provide an opportunity to address the second objection. In order to explore whether geography matters over and above individual-level characteristics, it is necessary to control for the relevant characteristics. The first phase of analysis will suggest what these individual—but geographically concentrated—characteristics are.

Defining Suburbia

Pointing to suburban diversity became an important means of critiquing the suburban-myth literature almost as soon as it appeared in the 1950s. By describing poor and working-class suburbs, authors such as Bennett Burger and Herbert Gans made important inroads against the dominant suburban mythology.[1] These challenges to the suburban myths have been widely accepted among political scientists and are used to explain the absence of suburbia from the current political science research agenda.[2] However, while it is certainly important to acknowledge the diversity of suburbia, the question remains open whether the term *suburb* is meaningless as a way of distinguishing between areas.

Zikmund argues in a 1973 article that while "we may speak . . . about suburbs in state and national politics, . . . the evidence of suburban diversity is so overwhelming as to make the discussion of a general suburban pattern both empirically inaccurate and theoretically misleading."[3] He then quotes Kramer: "the term 'suburb' has relatively little meaning. It refers only to a locality nearby and somehow interdependent with a city."[4] The question remains, however, whether this "meaningless" definition doesn't actually mean something. Is the suburb's nearness to a city such a meaningless feature?

Other observers acknowledge suburbia's diversity while at the same time underscoring the common feature of the suburban relationship to the city. Gerald Frug, for example, a professor of law who has written on the suburbs, notes that the diversity of areas labeled suburban may prevent them from having "a single unified interest."[5] At the same time, however, he also characterizes the suburb as an area that is defined in relation to a city. In the course of defining suburbs in this way, Frug quotes Robert Fishman's *Bourgeois Utopias*, a history of suburbanization.

> "Every true suburb," in Robert Fishman's words, "is the outcome of two opposing forces, an attraction toward the opportunities of the great city and a simultaneous repulsion against urban life." The suburbs would not be what they are without this love/hate relationship with the city: if the recent, extraordinary American migration to the suburbs were fully successful and the central city ceased to exist altogether, the character of the suburbs would be radically different. There would, for example, be no place for those excluded by exclusionary zoning to live except the suburbs.[6]

The point here is not to deny the diversity of areas labeled suburban but to suggest that areas with little in common—other than the fact that they are communities outside central cities—may still have enough in common to make them and their residents worth talking about.

Observers of today's suburbs acknowledge the diversity of suburbia before embarking on their analyses, and it is instructive to look at what they see as the commonalities among suburbs that make it possible to talk about them as a group. William Schneider, who has written about the importance of suburbanization as a political trend, argues that despite the diversity of suburban areas, suburbanites do have characteristics in common: they are property owners and consequently extremely tax sensitive. However, in addition to addressing individual-level characteristics, Schneider describes suburbanites in terms of their rejection of the city and their attempt to escape from its ills. As noted in chapter 2, he explains the choice to live in the suburbs as the choice of the private over the public—private space, private entertainment, and private government.[7]

This same argument appeared in a *New York Times* article examining the relationship between suburbanization and politics. After discussing the increasing diversity of areas labeled suburban, the *Times* concluded:

> Despite that diversity, many analysts say suburbanites have one thing in common. While 30 or 40 years ago they might have viewed themselves as the beneficiaries of government programs like the G.I. bill, low-interest housing subsidies, highways and

public schools, today they often feel that the Government picks their pockets for the benefit of others who have not worked as hard to realize the American dream. Peter Morrison of the Rand Institute said of today's suburbanites: "They've worked hard, and even though they are children of immigrants, they look at the world like a suburbanite who has a stake in the status quo." David Rusk, the former mayor of Albuquerque, N.M., who wrote *Cities without Suburbs*, said, "I suspect the black suburban voter is no more eager to see poor black households and subsidized renters move into his neighborhood than a white suburban voter."[8]

This same view of the distinguishing feature of suburban voters is found in Thomas Byrne Edsall and Mary D. Edsall's *Chain Reaction: The Impact of Race, Rights, and Taxes on American Politics*. Citing evidence from post-1988 focus groups, Edsall and Edsall found that a prevalent theme among Democrats who voted Republican was resistance to governmental programs that they perceived as having been designed to help others who, unlike themselves, had not worked hard.[9]

In his history of suburbanization, Kenneth Jackson begins by acknowledging the diversity of suburbia but argues that this is not the end of the story. Jackson notes that despite the differences between places like San Diego and Dallas on the one hand and Buffalo and Cleveland on the other, "one may nevertheless generalize about the American residential experience."

American metropolises do vary greatly.... But similarities among American residential patterns are much more numerous than are differences.... The essential similarities in American suburbanization become clear when we shift to an international perspective. The United States has thus far been unique in four important respects that can be summed up in the following sentence: affluent and middle-class Americans live in suburban areas that are far from their work places, in homes that they own, and in the center of yards that by urban standards elsewhere are enormous. This uniqueness thus involves population density, home-ownership, residential status, and journey-to-work.[10]

To make the point that it is possible to generalize about American metropolitan organization and suburbs, Jackson then compares the United States with European and former Eastern bloc countries.

What emerges from these accounts is an acknowledgment of suburban diversity that is accompanied by a belief that suburban areas have enough in common to make the term meaningful. While Kramer may feel that the defining characteristic of suburbia is "merely" its closeness to the central city, others argue that the very development of the suburb—near yet not "of" the city—tells us important things about the nature of the area and its inhabitants.

Once a term is used to refer to almost half the population, acknowledging the heterogeneity of the entity that it describes is unavoidable. The question remains, though, whether the term is necessarily rendered meaningless by this heterogeneity.[11] Although it is certainly true that the definition used here includes statistics for the suburbs of New York City and the suburbs of Altoona, Pennsylvania; the suburbs of Los Angeles and the suburbs of Owensboro, Kentucky, despite the diversity of the areas classified as suburban, the finding of consistent, significant differences between all suburbs and all cities would nevertheless be interesting. An analysis of 1990 census data can be used to explore in greater detail what these areas labeled suburban are really like—and how, if at all, they differ from cities.

Comparing Cities and Suburbs in Statistical Terms

The first difficulty encountered in trying to compare city and suburban areas statistically is that no universally agreed upon definition of a suburb exists. Although it does identify areas as "central city," the U.S. Census has steered clear of developing its own classification of suburban areas. Those who use census data to describe suburbs most often rely on census-defined metropolitan areas (MAs) as the basis for a definition of suburbia.[12] In this approach, suburbs are defined as those portions of MAs that lie outside the boundaries of the central city but within the boundaries of the MA.[13] The census definition of an MA—"a large population nucleus, together with adjacent communities that have a high degree of economic and social integration with that nucleus"—is a fairly good match for the contemporary understanding of the relationship between a city and its surrounding suburbs.[14]

Aggregate Comparisons

The first analysis will compare the characteristics of all central cities with those of all suburban areas. A suburban area will be defined here as the non–central-city portion of the MA, minus any rural portions of the MA. (With the aggregate metropolitan-area data, it is relatively easy to subtract the rural portions of the MA.)

At the time of the 1990 census, suburbs were home to 88.5 million people (36 percent of the population) and central cities to almost 78 million (31 percent of the population).[15] In terms of socioeconomic measures, suburbs are consistently better off than cities (table 1). The suburbs have a higher proportion of high school and college graduates, higher per capita and median household incomes, and higher rates of homeownership. In addition, they have a lower unemployment rate, a lower percentage of individuals and families living below the poverty line, and a lower percentage of children in single-parent families.

The differences in poverty and income statistics for suburban and urban areas are quite large; however, while unemployment is somewhat higher in cities, the difference is not huge—a pattern that suggests that the differences in income level reflect differences in job type. In particular, the higher percentage of the population without a high school education in the cities suggests that a higher proportion of the population is engaged in low-skill work. The smaller proportion of single-parent families in the suburbs also probably contributes to the difference in the percentage of families in poverty, although it does not explain it entirely, since the median income for female-headed households is also higher in the suburbs than in the cities—$17,000 versus $11,000.[16]

One observation that has been made about suburbs is that they are no longer "white." Although census data cannot be used to determine the degree of homogeneity within each suburb, it can be used to describe the overall distribution of population groups. As table 2 shows, the suburban population is not entirely made up of non-Hispanic whites; nevertheless, these figures also reveal that this is the only group that is underrepresented in the cities and overrepresented in the suburbs (in comparison with the percentage of non-Hispanic whites in the total population). While blacks and Hispanics are not completely missing from suburban areas, they are disproportionately found in cities rather than in suburbs.[17] And while blacks, Asians, and Hispanics make up only 20 percent of the suburban population, they make up over 40 percent of the city population. Of course, these figures do not tell us anything about the degree of homogeneity of individual suburbs—in other words, whether the 8 percent of the suburban population that is black lives in integrated suburbs or in all-black suburbs. But the literature on black suburbanization suggests that the latter is the case.

This picture of the racial composition of suburbs and cities is supported by Douglas Massey and Nancy Denton's findings in *American Apartheid: Segregation and the Making of the Underclass*. After careful analysis of 1980 census data, they conclude that

> during the 1970s, black-white segregation was maintained at high levels in most U.S. metropolitan areas, yielding high levels of racial isolation that were particularly intense within central cities. The characteristic pattern of black cities surrounded by white suburbs persisted. . . . Black suburbanization had begun in most metropolitan areas by 1980, but black entry into suburbs typically did not bring integration. On the contrary, suburban blacks experienced considerable segregation and isolation, both of which tended to be quite high in suburbs where blacks were represented in large numbers.[18]

While data from the 1990 census became available only shortly before the publication of their book, Massey and Denton's initial study of this data suggested that not much had changed since the 1980 census.[19]

More recent analyses of diversity in the suburbs paint a mixed picture. More blacks and Hispanics are now living in the suburbs of metropolitan America, and the numbers of all-white neighborhoods have declined. At the same time, however, suburban residents are disproportionately likely to be non-Hispanic whites, and the numbers of all-black neighborhoods have increased.[20] Furthermore, on the basis of his analysis of 1990 census data, Frey has suggested that patterns of immigration from Latin America and Asia, combined with new patterns of internal population movement, are also affecting the ethnic and racial makeup of metropolitan America: more ethnic and racial minorities are settling in the suburbs at the same time as other lines of division are emerging. "Distinct patterns of immigration and internal migration, along with evidence that an immigrant 'push' may be operating in several high immigration areas, appear to lay the groundwork for sharper geographic disparities in demographic composition for the US population."[21]

Another way to explore arguments that suburbanization is no longer a white-only phenomenon is to break down the differences between suburban and urban populations by race. As table 3 shows, both blacks and whites are better off, on average, in the suburbs than in the cities. However, black suburbanites are still worse off than white suburbanites. In addition, the difference that suburbanization makes in the income and poverty statistics for the black population is generally greater than the difference that suburbanization makes for whites. For example, black suburbanites have an unemployment rate of 9.4 percent, as compared with a rate of only 4.3 percent for white suburbanites. However, while the unemployment rate for white city dwellers is only slightly higher (0.9 percentage points) than that of their suburban counterparts, the difference in unemployment between black suburban and city populations is 5 percentage points. Similarly, only 4.3 percent of white suburban families live below the poverty line, while 16.1 percent of black suburban families do. But the difference between the percentage of suburban and urban white families living in poverty is 3.5 percentage points, while the difference in poverty rates between suburban and urban black families is 12 percentage points.

Looking only at the thirty-nine metropolitan areas with 1990 populations over 1 million, Frey finds similar patterns. Both blacks and Hispanics in the suburbs of these metropolitan areas have, on average, lower rates of graduation from college and lower mean household incomes than their white suburban counterparts.[22]

Two other characteristics that are sometimes considered important in defining suburbia are mobility and commuting patterns. With respect to mobility, suburban and city residents are equally likely to be living in the same state in which they were born (57 percent and 57 percent, respectively) and about equally likely to have lived in the same house for the past five years (52 percent and 50 percent, respectively). Suburbanites appear to be no more restless, on average, than city residents.[23]

Residents of cities and suburbs do differ, however, in their commuting patterns. While a suburban resident is commonly thought of as someone who drives to work in the city every day, table 4 shows that this is true only for a minority of suburbanites: a majority work in the same metropolitan area in which they live, but outside the central city. In contrast, a majority of city residents work within the city in which they live. These figures are in keeping with the claims made by some observers that the new suburbia—with its own shopping and employment centers as well as its own housing—is increasingly self-contained.[24] Again, in contrast to the image of suburbanites as commuters, statistics on commuting times also show that suburbanites do not spend more time commuting than their city counterparts, although they are much more likely to spend their commute in a car than on public transportation.

Comparisons by Size and Region

The aggregate comparisons presented so far group together all suburbs and all cities, regardless of the size of the metropolitan area or the region of the country in which it is located. This choice was deliberate, because the first question being explored was whether the simple dichotomy between suburb and city has any meaning. But comparing specific categories of suburb is also useful. Knowing to what extent these aggregate comparisons vary if only the largest metropolitan areas are considered helps identify city-suburb patterns in the large population centers that inform many popular conceptions of suburban America. Furthermore, comparing city-suburb differences across regions reveals how much these patterns vary with the location of the metropolitan area.

Patterns within the thirty-nine metropolitan areas with populations over 1 million do not seem to differ much from those reported for all metropolitan areas. For example, the suburbs of these large metropolitan areas are 80 percent non-Hispanic white and 7 percent black, compared with 80 percent non-Hispanic white and 8 percent black for all suburban areas. The cities of the largest thirty-nine are 52 percent non-Hispanic white and 25 percent black, compared with 59 percent non-Hispanic white and 22 percent black for all areas. The racial divide—differences between blacks and whites with respect to income, education, and other characteristics—appears somewhat starker when only the largest metropolitan areas are considered, but the inclusion of all areas does not appear to dilute these differences to any great degree.[25]

Variation across regions is apparent, however (table 5). Like those of the Northeast and Midwest, the suburbs of the South and West have higher percentages of non-Hispanic whites and fewer people living in poverty than their cities, but the suburbs of the South and West are more diverse than those in the Northeast and Midwest.

Suburbs in the South have higher percentages of blacks than those of other regions, and suburbs in the West include significant percentages of Hispanics and Asians. Furthermore, suburbs in both the South and the West have somewhat higher proportions of their populations living in poverty than those in the Northeast and Midwest.

These regional variations will become even more evident in the next section of the chapter, which turns from aggregate comparisons to variations across metropolitan areas.

Metropolitan-Level Comparisons

In contrast to the first analysis, in which the averages for all suburbs were compared with the averages for all cities, this analysis compares each city with its own suburban ring—here defined as the non–central-city portion of the metropolitan area.[26] While the aggregate statistics reveal consistent—though not necessarily large—differences between suburban and urban areas, the aggregation may conceal considerable variation within individual metropolitan areas. It is therefore important to understand not only how all cities differ from all suburbs but also how individual cities differ from their own suburban rings. Are city residents consistently economically worse off than residents of the surrounding suburbs, or is this true only for a few large metropolitan areas? Furthermore, are the racial, ethnic, and socioeconomic characteristics of all suburban rings fairly diverse?

The analyses designed to address these questions were based on census data that compare suburban rings to their particular central cities. The data are organized by metropolitan area—in most cases single metropolitan statistical areas, but in some cases consolidated metropolitan statistical areas (CMSAs).[27] The 1990 census designated a total of 283 MAs or CMSAs.

Because the data are organized differently at the level of individual MAs, it was not possible, for this segment of the analysis, to subtract those portions of the metropolitan area that are rural. Consequently, it is important to keep in mind the possible effect of including some primarily rural areas in what is being classified as suburbia. Because rural areas tend to be less densely populated than both cities and suburbs, including them as parts of suburbs exaggerates the extent to which suburbs are less densely populated than cities. The inclusion of rural areas within suburbs also underestimates the income and education differences between suburbs and cities because rural areas often have higher levels of poverty and lower levels of educational attainment than suburbs.[28]

The basis for the intrametropolitan comparisons is a socioeconomic city-suburb ratio for each city and its suburban ring; these ratios are based on many of the same socioeconomic variables that were used in the previous analyses. So, for example, the percentage of the population that is black in the suburbs of Boston was divided by the percentage of the population that is black in the city of Boston. A ratio of 1 indicates that the same percentage of the city and the suburban population is black; a ratio of less than 1 indicates that the percentage of blacks in the suburbs is smaller than that in the city; and a ratio of more than 1 indicates that the percentage of blacks in the suburbs is higher than that in the city.

Table 6 shows the average of these ratios across all metropolitan areas. (In other words, the ratios for each metropolitan area have been added together and divided by 283, the total number of areas included.) It appears from these ratios that, on average, the relationship between particular suburban areas and their central cities is the same as the relationship between the average of all suburban areas and all cities. The smallest city-suburb ratios across metropolitan areas are for the percentage of black residents, the percentage of female-headed households, and the percentage living in poverty. The largest ratio is for homeownership: residents of the suburbs are, on average, nearly one and one-half times more likely to own their own home than residents of the nearby city.

Interestingly, fairly substantial differences in two areas—the percentage living in poverty and the percentage living in female-headed households—do not translate into much difference in per capita income. The ratios for per capita income and education are essentially 1, indicating that, on average, city residents do not differ significantly from the residents of the surrounding suburbs on these measures. However, it is important to keep in mind that the density and education ratios are probably lower than they would have been if the rural areas in the MA had been excluded, and the poverty ratio is probably higher.

Turning now to the statistics for each metropolitan area, the picture that emerges is at once of suburban diversity and city-suburb inequality.[29] Despite variation in socioeconomic composition across suburban rings, within almost every metropolitan area, the suburban ring is better off than the central city it surrounds.

Density

Every suburban ring is much less densely populated than its central city. The city-suburb ratios for population density range from 0.001 (Casper, Wyoming) to 0.34 (Fort Myers–Cape Coral, Florida). Although these numbers are probably pushed down by the inclusion of some rural areas on the edges of suburban counties, the difference in density is still large. At the same time, a fair degree of diversity is apparent among suburban areas: several cities in Texas, for example, have suburban rings with densities of only 17 people per square mile, while the New York suburban area has a density of 1,321 people per square mile.

Race

In almost every metropolitan area, the majority of the black population lives in the city, not in the surrounding suburbs. All but two of the exceptions to this pattern have minuscule African American populations, with the percentage of African Americans about the same in the city as in the suburbs.[30] This finding is in keeping with those of Massey and Gross: from 1970 to 1980, "desegregation only occurred in those metropolitan areas where the number of blacks was relatively small."[31] Miami–Fort Lauderdale, Florida, and Tallahassee, Florida, have somewhat larger black populations—17.5 percent and 30 percent, respectively, and while neither city contains a clear majority of the area's black population, neither do the suburbs: in these two MAs, the percentage of blacks is about the same in the city as in the suburbs.[32]

While few suburban rings are as diverse as the cities they surround, a number are clearly more diverse than the popular image of suburbia would lead us to expect. Sixty-five MAs have populations that are less than 80 percent non-Hispanic white, and seventeen MAs have populations that are less than 60 percent non-Hispanic white. While the existence of sixty-five MAs with racially diverse populations offers evidence that the suburbs are not completely devoid of people of color, even in these MAs, every one of the suburbs—with one exception—is less diverse than its central city. Among these sixty-five MAs, twenty-seven of the cities differ in racial composition by fewer than 10 percentage points from their suburbs, while fourteen differ by 20 percentage points or more. In addition, the smaller the difference between the city and surrounding suburbs, the more likely it is that the population of color in the MA is Hispanic rather than black. Of the twenty-seven suburban areas that differ from their city by fewer than 10 percentage points, only eight have a mainly black minority population, while of the fourteen cities differing by 20 percentage points or more, twelve have a mainly black minority population. These numbers suggest that Hispanics are much less likely to be concentrated in the city portion of the MA. Instead, a large Hispanic population in an MA will tend to be distributed somewhat evenly between the city and suburbs. On the other hand, an MA with a large black population is much more likely to have that black population concentrated disproportionately in its central city. This finding is in keeping with those of Massey and Denton, who found that in no metropolitan area are Hispanics as strongly segregated as blacks.[33]

Poverty

The poverty rates in cities and suburban rings exhibit the same patterns as the other variables do: suburban diversity and city-suburb inequality. The percentage of the population living below the poverty line varies widely across suburban areas, from a high of 48 percent in the suburbs of Laredo, Texas, to a low of 3 percent in the suburbs of Waterbury, Connecticut. As expected, however, the percentage of the population living in poverty is almost always higher in cities than in their surrounding suburbs. Of 283 MAs, only 15 deviate from this pattern—and often not by very much.[34] Moreover, the MAs whose suburban rings are poorer, on average, than their cities include large rural areas within the metropolitan boundaries, which may account, in part, for the higher poverty rates in the suburbs. For example, in Bismarck, North Dakota; Fort Smith, Arkansas-Oklahoma; Las Cruces, New Mexico; and Visalia–Tulare–Porterville, California, almost half of the suburban populations are actually rural; and in Laredo, Texas, almost all of the suburban population is. In another 24 MAs, the differences between city and suburban poverty rates are at or close to zero, which leaves 244 MAs in which the city is poorer than the surrounding suburban areas.[35]

The relatively small city-suburb differences found in the MAs whose suburbs are, on average, poorer than their cities can be contrasted with city-suburb differences in MAs where the city is poorer. For example, the poverty rate in Atlanta, Georgia, is 3.5 times greater than in the suburbs; in Detroit–Ann Arbor, Michigan, 4.5 times greater; in Hartford and New Britain, Connecticut, over 5 times greater.

Unemployment

A look at unemployment rates for cities and suburbs reveals, not surprisingly, a pattern that is similar to that for poverty rates. The variation in unemployment rates among suburban areas is less pronounced than the variation in poverty rates; nevertheless, unemployment varies from a high of 16 percent in the suburban ring of McAllen–Edinburg–Mission, in Texas, to a low of 2 percent in the suburbs of Lincoln, Nebraska.

Variation between suburban rings and their cities is also less pronounced for unemployment than for poverty rates: in sixty-nine metropolitan areas, the suburbs have, on average, approximately the same unemployment rate as their central city. This finding is in keeping with the aggregate analysis, which showed a larger city-suburb differential for poverty rates than for unemployment. However, as with poverty rates, few suburban rings—only twelve—have substantially higher unemployment rates, on average, than their cities.[36] Seven of these MAs are also among the areas in which the poverty rate is higher in the suburbs, and seven are located either in California or Texas.

Of the MAs whose unemployment rates are higher in the suburbs than in their cities, only three have city-suburb differences of more than 4 percentage points. On the other hand, in thirty-nine of the remaining MAs, the unemployment rate in the central city is more than 4 percentage points higher than in the suburbs. Three of the biggest differentials are found in Michigan MAs: Benton Harbor has an unemployment rate of 29 percent, compared with a suburban rate of 6.2 percent; Detroit–Ann Arbor has an unemployment rate of 16.4 percent, compared with a suburban rate of 5.9 percent; and Flint has an unemployment rate of 18.3 percent, compared with a suburban rate of 7.9 percent. Again, there is variation across suburban rings, but the general tendency is for cities to be surrounded by suburban rings with lower levels of unemployment and poverty.

Homeownership

The one statistic on which almost no exception to the prevailing tendency can be found is homeownership: suburban rings always contain a higher percentage of homeowners than do their central cities. The only exception to this pattern is Naples, Florida. The central-city population of Naples is very small—only 19,000—and it appears to be a relatively prosperous city with a slightly lower poverty rate than its suburbs and an unemployment rate that is no higher than that of the suburbs. The highest ratio of suburb-to-city homeownership rates is in the New York CMSA, where suburban housing units are 2.4 times more likely to be owner occupied than city housing units, and the difference between city and suburban homeownership rates is over 41 percentage points.

City-suburb statistics on homeownership seem to lend support to Schneider's argument that homeownership is the distinguishing feature of suburbanites. However, it is worth noting that even in New York, where the city-suburb divergence on this measure is so strong, 30 percent of city dwellers are homeowners and 30 percent of suburban residents are not.

Commuting

As the aggregate statistics suggest, the idea that most suburban residents commute to jobs in the city is not an accurate description of most metropolitan areas. Of 283 metropolitan areas, in only 64 does more than 50 percent of the suburban workforce commute into the central city. The area in which the highest proportion of suburban workers—75 percent—commutes to the city is Topeka, Kansas. However, no other MA comes close to this level: in most areas in which a majority of suburbanites work in the city, this majority is only in the 50 percent to low 60 percent range.

In marked contrast to the pattern in Topeka, only 7 percent of suburban workers in the New York metropolitan area work in the city—a statistic that offers support for the view that unlike those of previous decades, the suburbs of today are no longer primarily bedroom communities that supply workers for the city. Indeed, Frey and Speare's analysis of 1980 census data found that in the largest metropolitan areas, the percentage of the workforce living in the suburbs and working in the city had declined since the 1970s, while the percentage of the workforce living and working in the suburbs had increased.[37] Today's suburban resident quite probably works, as well as lives, in the suburbs—making possible, as noted earlier, a more complete disconnection from the city.

Characteristics of Healthier Cities

In the past, some analysts have argued that the pattern in which a central city has more poverty and more racial and ethnic minorities than its suburbs holds true primarily for large and old cities.[38] However, census data demonstrate that while age is an important predictor of which cities follow this pattern, size is not. Most of the cities that do not differ significantly from their suburban rings with respect to racial and ethnic composition, poverty rates, and unemployment rates are indeed relatively small: for example, Yuma City, Arizona, has a population of 27,437, and Glens Falls, New York, has a population of 15,023. However, this group of cities also includes a number of large cities: Albuquerque, New Mexico, for example, has a population of 384,736, and Bakersfield, California, has a population of 368,657. In addition, many small cities do, in fact, follow the more typical pattern. Finally, the list of cities that do not follow the typical pattern—whether small or large cities—is not extensive.

It is, however, true that most cities that are exceptions—that is, most cities that have lower poverty levels, lower unemployment, and fewer minorities than their surrounding suburbs—are newer cities. In particular, the bigger cities that are exceptions (like Albuquerque and Bakersfield) tend to be in the South and West rather than in the older urban areas of the Northeast and Midwest. Almost all the exceptions to the standard city-suburban pattern are metropolitan areas located in the South and the West; this finding is in keeping with the earlier aggregate analysis, which illustrated that suburbs and cities in these two regions diverge less on various socioeconomic measures than do suburbs and cities in the Northeast and Midwest. These regional differences can probably be explained by differences in development history and annexation practices, which have allowed some of these newer cities in the South and West to retain more of the metropolitan area's population growth and commercial development than the older cities in the Frost Belt.[39]

Summary

This statistical portrait of suburbia has revealed two main points: First, on a number of measures, suburban rings exhibit a large degree of diversity both within themselves and in relation to each other. Some suburban areas do indeed match the popular image of suburbia—primarily middle class, primarily white—but other suburban rings have ethnically and racially diverse populations, significant numbers of poor people, or both. Second, the prevailing pattern within metropolitan areas is that of suburban rings with fewer poor people, fewer racial and ethnic minorities, lower unemployment, and more home-owners than the cities they surround.

These findings have two consequences for this study of suburban politics. First, it is possible to use the term *suburb* as though it has some meaning—at least as much meaning as the term *city*. Suburban diversity is a fact, but this does not mean that residents of suburban rings show no general tendencies that differ from those of central city residents. However, to say anything meaningful about suburbia today and the politics of its residents, it is necessary to take diversity into account and to observe how it is related to variation in the attitudes of suburban dwellers.

Notes

1. Bennet M. Berger, *Working-Class Suburb* (Berkeley and Los Angeles: University of California Press, 1960); Herbert J. Gans, *The Levittowners* (New York: Pantheon Books, 1967).

2. Louis H. Masotti, "Prologue: Suburbia Reconsidered—Myth and Counter-Myth," in *The Urbanization of the Suburbs*, ed. Louis H. Masotti and Jeffrey K. Hadden (Beverly Hills, Calif.: Sage Publications, 1973).

3. Joseph Zikmund II, "Suburbs in State and National Politics," in Masotti and Hadden, *Urbanization of the Suburbs.*

4. John Kramer, *North American Suburbs: Politics, Diversity, and Change* (Berkeley, Calif.: Glendessary Press, 1972), xv.

5. Gerald E. Frug, "Decentering Decentralization," *University of Chicago Law Review* 60, no. 2 (spring 1993):291.

6. Ibid.

7. William Schneider, "The Suburban Century Begins: The Real Meaning of the 1992 Election," *Atlantic Monthly*, July 1992.

8. Karen De Witt, "Suburbs, Especially in the South, Are Becoming the Source of Political Power in the U.S.," *New York Times*, 19 December 1994, p. B9.

9. Thomas Byrne Edsall and Mary D. Edsall, *Chain Reaction: The Impact of Race, Rights, and Taxes on American Politics* (New York: W.W. Norton, 1992), 226.

10. Kenneth T. Jackson, *Crabgrass Frontier: The Suburbanization of the United States* (Oxford: Oxford University Press, 1985), 6.

11. For example, the terms *male* and *female* refer to two categories, each of which encompasses roughly half the population and clearly contains a great deal of heterogeneity. The terms are meaningful nevertheless.

12. For a discussion of the relative merits of different ways of classifying areas as suburban, see David C. Huckabee, "Congressional Districts of the 99th Congress Classified on an Urban to Rural Continuum" (report prepared for the Congressional Research Service, 9 September 1985).

13. See, for example, *American National Election Studies, 1948–1994* (Ann Arbor, Mich.: Inter-University Consortium for Political and Social Research, 1995); Katherine L. Bradbury, Anthony Downs, and Kenneth A. Small, *Urban Decline and the Future of American Cities* (Washington, D.C.: Brookings Institution Press, 1982); "Suburbs: Potential but Unrealized House Influence," *Congressional Quarterly Weekly Report*, 6 April 1974; William H. Frey and Alden Speare Jr., *Regional and Metropolitan Growth and Decline in the United States* (New York: Russell Sage Foundation, 1988); Peter O. Muller, *Contemporary Suburban America* (Englewood Cliffs, N.J.: Prentice-Hall, 1981), 4–6; Frederick M. Wirt et al., *On the City's Rim: Politics and Policy in Suburbia* (Lexington, Mass.: D.C. Heath, 1972).

14. The more technical portion of the definition is as follows: "Each MA must contain either a place with a minimum population of 50,000 or a Census Bureau–defined urbanized area and a total MA population of at least 100,000 (75,000 in New England). An MA also may include one or more outlying counties that have close economic and social relationships with the central county. An outlying county must have a specified level of commuting to the central counties and also must meet certain standards regarding metropolitan character, such as population density, urban population and population growth." Bureau of the Census, *1990 Census of Population and Housing. Supplementary Reports* (Washington, D.C.: GPO, December 1993). The main problem with this definition is that except for New England, where metropolitan areas are defined along town lines, the census defines metropolitan areas by county. Since some of the outlying portions of the counties included within the MAs are primarily rural, this means of defining suburbs somewhat exaggerates the suburban population and may give a slightly inaccurate impression of who is living there. There are two ways to compensate for this problem: the first is, when possible, to subtract the nonurbanized portion of the MA from the totals. However, this approach does not address the fact that some of this nonurbanized portion of the MA may well contain communities that are more suburblike than rural. The other alternative is simply to be conscious of the ways in which the inclusion of some rural areas will affect the statistics for the MA and its suburbs.

15. When urbanized areas outside of metropolitan areas are included in the definition of a suburb, then the number of people living in the suburbs rises to 109 million—44 percent of the population. This figure is closer to the widely heralded figure of 50 percent suburban population (see Schneider, "Suburban Century Begins").

16. Bureau of the Census, *1990 Census of Population. Social and Economic Characteristics* (Washington, D.C.: GPO, 1993), table 23.

17. The term *Hispanic* is used in discussions of census data because that is the term used by the Census Bureau.

18. Douglas S. Massey and Nancy A. Denton, *American Apartheid: Segregation and the Making of the American Underclass* (Cambridge, Mass.: Harvard University Press, 1993), 73–74.

19. Ibid., 221–23.

20. David Cutler and Jacob Vigdor, "The Rise of a Suburban Ghetto? Trends and Costs for African-American Families" (paper presented at the Suburban Racial Change Conference, Harvard University, Cambridge, Mass., 28 March 1998); Nancy A. Denton and Richard Alba, "Suburban Racial and Ethnic Change at the Neighborhood Level: The Declining Number of All-White Neighborhoods" (paper presented at the Suburban Racial Change Conference, Harvard University, Cambridge, Mass., 28 March 1998); William H. Frey and Douglas Geverdt, "Changing Suburban Demographics: Beyond the 'Black-White, City-Suburb' Typology" (paper presented at the Suburban Racial Change Conference, Harvard University, Cambridge, Mass., 28 March 1998).

21. William H. Frey, "Immigration, Domestic Migration, and Demographic Balkanization in America: New Evidence for the 1990s," *Population and Development Review* 22, no. 4 (December 1996):756.

22. Frey and Geverdt, "Changing Suburban Demographics," 6.

23. Bureau of the Census, *1990 Census of Population* (Washington, D.C.: GPO, 1992), table 18.

24. Joel Garreau, *Edge City: Life on the New Frontier* (New York: Doubleday, 1991).

25. Bureau of the Census, *1990 Census of Population. General Population Characteristics. Metropolitan Areas* (Washington, D.C.: GPO, November 1992), tables 1, 4, and 11.

26. While comparing each individual suburb to its city would provide a more complete picture of city-suburb differences, the huge number of individual communities and the organization of the census data make this unrealistic. Thus, because the analysis is based on statistics for suburban rings rather than for individual suburbs, it will reveal variation among suburbs across metropolitan areas, but it cannot illustrate variation among suburbs within a single metropolitan area.

27. The census uses this term to refer to areas that have populations of over 1 million and that can be subdivided into smaller PMSAs (primary metropolitan statistical areas) but that exhibit enough integration to be considered one area.

28. In order to capture the heterogeneity of suburban rings, Frey and Geverdt have suggested a typology of metropolitan-area communities that distinguishes between inner and outer employment centers, inner and outer residential suburbs, and low-density areas. While this is certainly a useful and important way of thinking about the diversity of suburbia, Frey's analysis of Los Angeles, Detroit, and Atlanta—which used this typology—suggests that although diversity does exist within the suburban rings, the central city still contains the highest proportions of racial and ethnic minorities and the highest levels of poverty. Frey and Geverdt, "Changing Suburban Demographics."

29. The data for individual metropolitan areas were calculated on the basis of information in Bureau of the Census, *1990 Census of Population and Housing,* summary tape file 3C, 1992.

30. Glens Falls, New York; Grand Forks, North Dakota; Great Falls, Montana; Honolulu, Hawaii; Rapid City, South Dakota; Wausau, Wisconsin; and Yuba City, California.

31. Douglas S. Massey and Andrew B. Gross, "Explaining Trends in Residential Segregation, 1970–1980," *Urban Affairs Quarterly* 27, no. 1 (September 1991):13–15. See also Massey and Denton, *American Apartheid,* 112.

32. Again, it is important to keep in mind that these figures do not reveal anything about how diverse particular suburbs within an MA are. An MA may have a suburban ring with a 30 percent minority population, but it is not clear whether that 30 percent is concentrated in one or two all-minority suburbs or is spread evenly throughout the suburbs.

33. Massey and Denton, *American Apartheid,* 77.

34. In the following cities, the percentage of those living below the poverty line is smaller than in the suburban rings (the difference between the suburb and the city is in parentheses): Laredo, Texas (11.54); McAllen–Edinburg–Mission, Texas (11.14); El Paso, Texas (9.62); Yuba, Arizona (7.26); Las Cruces, New Mexico (6.02); Corpus Christi, Texas (6.01); Naples, Florida (4.87); Odessa, Texas (4.18); Fort Smith, Arkansas–Oklahoma (3.94); Visalia–Tulare–Porterville, California (3.87); Albuquerque, New Mexico (2.88); Modesto, California (2.51); Bakersfield, California (2.48); Bismarck, North Dakota (2.37); Decatur, Alabama (2.07). Bureau of the Census, *1990 Census of Population and Housing,* summary tape file 3C.

35. It is interesting to note that among the MAs in which city income is higher than suburban income, those with greatest city-suburb differential are all located in Texas. This may be because Texas cities have been very successful at annexing their surrounding suburbs, drawing wealthier areas inside the city boundaries. It may also be because significant portions of Texas MAs tend to be quite rural, and the suburban poverty measure therefore includes a fair amount of rural poverty.

36. The following cities have lower unemployment rates than their suburban rings (the difference between the city and the suburb is in parentheses): Yuma, Arizona (7.41); Laredo, Texas (4.61); McAllen–Edinburg–Mission, Texas (4.33); Visalia–Tulare–Porterville, California (3.86); Bakersfield, California (3.73); Modesto, California (2.62); Wheeling, West Virginia (2.62); Fresno, California (2.06); Casper, Wyoming (1.96); El Paso, Texas (1.49); Biloxi–Gulfport, Mississippi (1.41); Duluth, Minnesota-Wisconsin (1.27). Bureau of the Census, *1990 Census of Population and Housing,* summary tape file 3C.

37. William H. Frey and Alden Speare Jr., *Regional and Metropolitan Growth and Decline in the United States* (New York: Russell Sage Foundation, 1988), 392–98.

38. Leo F. Schnore, "The Socioeconomic Status of Cities and Suburbs," *American Sociological Review* 28, no. 1 (February 1963); Wirt et al., *On the City's Rim.*

39. Frey and Speare, *Growth and Decline,* 183–84.

CHAPTER FOUR

Laying the Groundwork: Methodological Issues

The previous two chapters explored current perspectives on what constitutes a suburb and on whether suburbanites have distinctive political attitudes. The next two chapters will use these perspectives as the basis for a statistical analysis of public opinion data, which will then be used to explore differences in the politics of city and suburban dwellers. This chapter lays the groundwork for the statistical analysis to come.

The two major points of contention in the discussion of suburban politics are these: First, do suburbanites have unique political views that are conditioned by where they live, or are these views related to individual-level characteristics that would operate in the same way no matter where the respondent lived? Second, are suburbs and the people who live there so diverse as to render any generalizations meaningless?

Chapter 5 tackles the first question by exploring the relationship between public opinion and the location of respondents, while controlling for individual-level characteristics. The analysis relies on National Election Study (NES) data from 1952 to 1992, which is particularly useful for several reasons: first, it includes answers to questions about national politics that were asked repeatedly over a long time span; second, it contains detailed socioeconomic information about respondents; third—and, for the purposes of this discussion, most important—it includes information about whether respondents lived in cities, suburbs, or rural areas.

Chapter 6 addresses the second question by considering variation among suburban rings and the cities they surround. While the analysis of public opinion data in chapter 5 treats the undifferentiated city-suburb categories as meaningful, the analysis in chapter 6 acknowledges the significant diversity of areas labeled suburban. Combining census data with the NES data makes it possible to categorize respondents not only according to whether they live in a suburban area but also according to the kind of suburban area it is—which, in turn, makes possible a more nuanced understanding of the relationship between local context and political attitudes.

Choice and Formulation of Variables

Since the analysis that follows involves the repeated use of the same independent and dependent variables, it will be useful to discuss their choice and formulation here. All the variables were drawn from National Election Studies. Those described as representing the contemporary period come from three surveys pooled together for the years 1988, 1990, and 1992: these years correspond most closely to the beginning of recent discussions about the political relevance of suburbanization and to the time period when the 1990 census data was collected. National Election Studies from 1954 to 1992 are used for the historical analysis of suburban political behavior over time.

Independent Variables

The analysis relies on a number of different dependent variables, each of which is regressed on the same set of independent variables.[1] The independent variables include individual-level socioeconomic characteristics that are expected to be related to political opinion and behavior: party identification, age, income, education, gender, and race.[2] It may be that suburban residents differ politically from city residents only to the extent that suburbanites are more likely to be white and middle class. Because contextual explanations are regarded skeptically until individual-level explanations have been exhausted, it is important to include as many plausibly relevant individual-level characteristics as possible.

Some observers have suggested that the distinctiveness of suburban residents may not derive from basic socioeconomic indicators but may nevertheless involve individual-level rather than community-level characteristics. Consequently, two variables have been included that could arguably be the relevant characteristics behind the political impact of suburbanization: owning a home and being married with children. Homeownership and two-parent families are more prevalent in suburbs than in cities and may contribute to more conservative political attitudes.

Through dummy variables for being Jewish and being Catholic, the analysis also controls for religious belief. This was done in part to replicate earlier studies of suburban public opinion that included controls for religion, and in part because it seemed plausible that the distinctiveness of suburban politics could be driven by religious belief if members of certain denominations are more or less likely to live in the suburbs.[3] Finally, the analysis included a control variable for living in the South: the South has historically been associated with distinctive voting patterns, and suburbanization has been particularly prevalent in the South.

The inclusion of party identification as a control variable is complicated by the question of whether it is an exogenous or endogenous variable. If party identification is a fixed characteristic that is formed early in life and later influences an individual's stance on policy issues, then it is an important control variable. If, however, party identification is a choice influenced by policy stances and socioeconomic characteristics, then it should be treated (as it was in earlier studies of suburbanization) as a dependent variable. Consequently, the models were run both with and without party identification as an independent variable. The results for the models that include party identification as a control (the strongest test for the contextual variable) will usually be reported, and the results of the models run without this control will sometimes be reported. In addition, the analysis will treat party identification as a dependent variable and consider the possibility that living in a suburb has both a direct and an indirect effect (mediated through party identification) on the other dependent variables.

The formulation of the suburban-location variable was complicated by the issue of rural residents. The NES reports whether respondents reside (1) in an inner city, (2) in a suburb—that is, within the standard metropolitan area but outside the city, or (3) in a rural area—that is, outside the standard metropolitan area. One possibility was to create a dichotomous variable (assigning living in a suburb a code of 1 and not living in a suburb—i.e., living in a city or rural area—a code of 0). However, it is from urban areas that suburbs draw their population, and it is the suburbs' relationship to nearby urban areas that interests most observers of suburbs. Lumping urban and rural respondents together may mask the distinction between urban and suburban voters. Consequently, rural residents were excluded from the analysis.

Dependent Variables

The selection of dependent variables was based on the characteristics that are typically mentioned in current arguments about the effects of suburbanization. Since earlier studies of suburbanization often looked at vote choice, and since the significance of suburban voters was a theme of many discussions of the 1992 campaign, the first dependent variables considered are party identification and support for political candidates in presidential and congressional races. For the historical analysis, these are the only three dependent variables used because they are the only three questions asked consistently from the 1950s to the 1990s.

For the contemporary period, however, it was possible to explore the relationship between location and a wider variety of variables. The first variables considered for the contemporary period were the same as those considered for the historical period: presidential votes in 1988 and 1992, as well as 1992 support for Ross Perot, since the claim was often made that his supporters were disproportionately drawn from the suburbs. Votes for congressional candidates were also used as a dependent variable, although location was not expected to have an effect on any dichotomous (Democrat–Republican) vote choice. Given the earlier research on suburbanization, the hypothesis was that suburbanites, once socioeconomic variables are controlled for, are no more likely than city residents to vote for Republicans. Significant city-suburban differences were expected to emerge in policy preferences, but not in vote choice.

Consequently, in addition to vote choice variables, responses to a number of questions about federal spending were used as dependent variables. The questions—which concerned whether the federal government should spend more, the same, or less on particular programs—were chosen because they reflected arguments made about the impact of suburbanization. In each case, responses were coded on a scale of 1 to 3, with 1 representing a spending decrease, 2 representing no change in spending, and 3 representing a spending increase.

The first and most obvious of these is support for aid to cities.[4] In keeping with the argument that living in a suburb changes residents' self-interest, suburbanites were expected to be less supportive of federal aid to cities—first, because they receive less information about the problems of cities than they do about problems closer to hand, and second, because they do not directly benefit from aid to cities.[5]

Other dependent variables were drawn from discussions—by commentators such as William Schneider and Edsall and Edsall—about the significance of suburbanization. Schneider has argued that suburbanization is the choice of the private over the public and that suburbanites are distinctive in that (1) they favor fewer taxes and less government and (2) believe that people should take care of themselves without help from government.[6] Similarly, Edsall and Edsall have argued that suburbanization has allowed individuals to satisfy their desire for some increased services "through increased suburban and county expenditures, guaranteeing to themselves the highest possible tax return on their dollars, while continuing to maintain policies of fiscal conservatism at the federal level."[7] Consequently, opinion about spending on food stamps and on programs to help blacks were used as dependent variables; also included was a "feeling thermometer" question that asked respondents how close (on a scale of 0 to 100) they feel to welfare recipients. These questions all involve federal expenditures to assist poor people—something that suburbanites, isolated and secure in their nonurban communities, might not support.

According to contemporary arguments about suburbanization, living in a suburb should affect opinion on poverty programs. If you are not poor and live only among other people who are not poor, you may not feel that it is in your interest for the government to spend tax dollars on poverty programs; whereas if you are not poor and live among some people who are, you may feel that such programs are in your interest because they improve the quality of the community in which you live. In addition, people who live away from urban blight will have access to different kinds of information than those living in central cities when making political judgments about government spending levels. This distinction is particularly relevant when voters think about the appropriate level of government for social service provision. Even if those who reside in wealthier communities are not opposed to social spending, they may be more likely to favor local rather than federal spending. Elsewhere in the book, it is argued that the devolution of social policy is more attractive to residents of communities that have substantial resources and few needs than to those in more needy communities. Since the questions treated here as dependent variables have to do with federal policies, living in a suburb was expected to be associated with declining support for spending on these programs.

Opinion on Social Security spending was also included; even though this program is seen as benefiting the middle class as well as the poor, it does represent government action to help individuals. Similarly, the impact of living in a suburb on support for government spending in general was tested for, in order to see whether lack of support for spending stems from the fact that it is perceived as benefiting "other people"—the poor and racial minorities—or because of a more general opposition to federal spending. This question is of particular interest because it explicitly connects a decrease in spending with cuts in services. The responses were on a scale from 1 to 7, with 1 indicating agreement with the statement that "the government should provide many fewer services and reduce spending a lot" and 7 indicating agreement with the statement that "the government should provide many more services and increase spending a lot."

Causality

While the statistical analysis that follows can assess whether suburban residents have political attitudes that distinguish them from city residents, it cannot determine whether living in a suburb *causes* these distinctive attitudes or is merely associated with them. It may be that suburban residents have distinctive attitudes because of their experiences living in a suburb, or it may be that people with these particular attitudes self-select into suburbs.

Possible Approaches

The best way to deal with the question of causality would be to create a data set based on interviews with city dwellers who would then be re-interviewed once they moved to a suburb.[8] One of the NES panel studies at first appeared to have approximated such a data set: the same people were re-interviewed several times over a period of a few years, and any change in their residence was recorded. However, the extremely small number of respondents who moved from a city to a suburb during the panel study made this approach infeasible.

Another approach would involve using length of residence in the suburb as a proxy for influence. If those who have been in a suburb longer are the most likely to exhibit the distinctive politics of suburbia, this would lend support to the argument that a process of causation rather than self-selection is at work. However, in order for this argument to make sense, it would be necessary to know where people had moved from: if they had moved from one suburb to another, similar suburb, then the relevant factor would not be the length of time in the second suburb but the total length of time in a suburb. Unfortunately, information about where people had moved from was available only for the fewer than 2 percent of respondents who had been living in their current community for less than two years.

When data on mobility from the 1990 census are considered, the risks of ignoring the nature of a respondent's previous residence become obvious. Of the 46 percent of suburban dwellers in 1990 who had moved within the past five years to their current address, only 29 percent had previously resided in a central city. Similarly, among the 50 percent of city residents who had lived at a different address within the past five years, only 22 percent had lived in a suburb.[9] The fact that it cannot be assumed that recent arrivals in any particular suburban area are new arrivals to suburbia in general thus complicates any attempt to use length of residence to explore causality.

Another possible approach to the question of causality is the use of an instrumental variable. In this case, however, finding a satisfactory instrument—one that is correlated with the decision to move to the suburbs but not with the dependent variables (vote choice, party identification, and public opinion) is quite difficult. One choice that has been used in previous studies of urbanization—commuting time to the central city—appeared much less useful in the current context, which finds a minority of residents in most suburbs commuting to the city for work.

However, two variables that are used in chapter 6 to distinguish among suburban areas—the number of governments within the metropolitan area and the age of the metropolitan area—may help to address the question of causality. While within a given metropolitan area the decision to move to the suburbs rather than to the city may be correlated with political attitudes, the decision over *which* metropolitan area to move to is much more likely to be related to job opportunities or family proximity.[10] Consequently, a finding that city and suburban residents differ more from each other in older metropolitan areas and in metropolitan areas with lots of governments indicates that something about the experience of living in this kind of suburban area is affecting the political choices and attitudes of residents *after* they move.

Unfortunately, an alternative hypothesis cannot be dismissed: namely, the more communities there are in a metropolitan area, the greater the likelihood that the area offers an alternative that is more attractive than the city in terms of service provision and tax burden. Consequently, in metropolitan areas with large numbers of governments, the geographic sorting of residents may occur more efficiently, which may result in the greater divergence in political attitudes between suburban and city dwellers in these areas. Because age of metropolitan areas is correlated with the number of governments, the same concern applies.

Opposing Arguments

Since the use of metropolitan context may not answer the causality question conclusively, it is important to consider the opposing arguments in some detail. First, what about the argument that people who have particular attitudes self-select into suburbs, and that an identifiable suburban politics results from this self-selection rather than from the common experience of living in suburbia?

This argument is initially quite plausible. While it is probably rare for people to choose to live in a particular community specifically because of the political orientation of its residents, it is not uncommon for them to choose localities on the basis of factors that are almost certainly correlated with political orientation.[11] For example, Frey and Speare found in their study of metropolitan areas in the 1980s that

people were most likely to move to the suburbs where the tax disparity between the city and the rest of the metropolitan area was high,
where the city had a predominantly black population, and—in keeping with Tiebout—where the existence of a large number of communities offered a range of alternatives to the city's mix of taxes and
services.[12] It certainly seems plausible that the choice of locality on the
basis of the race of inhabitants, service provision, and tax burden is
correlated with political attitudes.

On the other hand, this argument leaves open the question of
what generates these preferences if they are not environmentally
derived. Wirt et al. argued in the early 1970s that

> our failure to find measurable independent locale effects on atti-
> tudes, once we have "partialled-out" the effects of individual
> attributes, suggests that the dynamics of attitude formation in
> urban and suburban populations are the same. The suburban
> "climate of opinion," while different from that of the city, does not
> seem to play a significant role in determining individual political
> orientations. Suburbanites' attitudes are different from those of
> their urban counterparts because of the kinds of people they are,
> *not* because of where they live.[13]

Wirt et al. argue that the lack of a significant difference between
urban and suburban dwellers, once individual characteristics are
taken into account, demonstrates the lack of a real contextual effect.
This perspective seems to assume that the socioeconomic characteristics of individuals are the mechanisms behind self-selection into
suburbs.

However, these variables are already controlled for in the current
analysis, which still finds a significant difference between respondents
on the basis of location. The following question then remains: If
preexisting attitudes cause self-selection into suburbs, where do these
preexisting attitudes come from, given that the most obvious
source—socioeconomic characteristics—has already been controlled
for?

In thinking about this question, it should also be kept in mind
that the process of suburbanization has continued steadily in the
United States since the end of the Second World War and has not
fluctuated during periods of increased liberalism or increased conservatism. Moreover, much work has documented the role of gov-

ernment in perpetuating suburbanization. The choice to move to the suburbs from the city has not been purely an instance of consumer choice. Deliberate government policies—federal mortgage guarantees, which favored the purchase of new suburban homes; federal housing policies, which maintained racial segregation; the federal highway program, which opened peripheral areas to development; and tax benefits for homeownership, which disproportionately aided suburbanites—ensured that when the decision to move to the suburbs was considered, the arguments would weigh in on the side of moving.

In addition, McKenzie, in his discussion of common-interest developments (CIDs), underscores ways in which the choice of where to live is not a straightforward instance of consumer preference—partly because, McKenzie argues, the building industry has played a central role in generating demand for a product that is profitable to build. "Given a great deal of latitude, the real estate industry followed the path of greatest profit and created suburbia and the consumer product we know as CID housing. At the same time, the industry worked hard to create and sustain a market for that product."[14] The role of consumer choice is also mitigated by the increasing prevalence of CID housing. McKenzie cites a study by the Advisory Commission on Intergovernmental Relations: "As CIDs spread, and as old housing is replaced by new CID housing, consumer choice is increasingly restricted. In short, growing numbers of Americans who wish to purchase new houses are going to be living in CIDs, and under the rule of private governments, regardless of their preferences."[15]

Indeed, the element of choice involved in location is also called into question by *Newsweek* and *New York Times* surveys that found large numbers of city dwellers unhappy about living in a city.[16] These findings suggest that factors other than inhabitants' differing preferences are involved in the sorting of populations into cities and suburbs. These surveys also found that increasing numbers of suburban residents have never lived in the city, which raises further issues concerning causality. The question of whether people move because they are different or are different because they move is less relevant when people are increasingly likely to have always lived in the suburbs. This discussion is not intended to suggest that people's locational choices do not in some sense represent their preferences; instead, it is meant to illustrate the complexity of the arguments on both sides of the causality question.

Because it seems clear that political attitudes are affected by a combination of individual and contextual characteristics, the inability of the current analysis to conclusively demonstrate the causal link between suburban living and distinctive political views is not overly troubling. The assumption in this volume is that even if the distinctive politics associated with living in a suburb resulted from self-selection rather than from exposure to a particular environment, the findings presented here are still interesting and important. First, an unexpected correlation was discovered between living (or choosing to live) in the suburbs and political opinion. According to earlier political science research on suburbanization, self-selection into suburbs was not associated with a distinctive politics. Second, suburbanization is increasing—so whichever way the causal relationship works, the relationship will become more important over time. Third, the sorting of individuals with similar political preferences into geographic clumps is significant in a political system that provides representation on the basis of geography.[17]

Finally, even if causality does work in the opposite direction—that is, even if distinctive attitudes *cause* people to move to the suburbs—these attitudes are still unavoidably affected by the existence of suburbs as a locational choice. Huckfeldt suggests just such an effect in his research on support for ethnic politicians among residents of ethnic neighborhoods. He explains why treating self-selection and contextual effects as mutually exclusive makes for a less than satisfactory approach to the study of political behavior:

> Self-selection actually constitutes a rather complex contextual argument. People choose to live in neighborhoods (when they have the freedom to choose) because they are attracted to them or repelled by other residential alternatives. Both the attraction and the repulsion are, at least in part, contextually based. Thus, we are not faced with an either-or situation. Both individual-level characteristics and contextual factors are important to an understanding of political behavior; their interaction produces a complex web of choices and reactions that are rooted in the personality of the actor and in the characteristics of others in the actor's environment.[18]

The existence of suburbs makes defection from the problems of the city possible by reinforcing the idea that the problems can be escaped without serious investment in solving them. It may be that people who are already less supportive of federal programs choose to live in the suburbs, rather than that people who live in the suburbs become less supportive of federal programs. However, the ability of these people to sort themselves out into homogeneous communities may allow these views to be perpetuated and strengthened in ways that would not be possible if the views were not associated with residential choice. It may be easier to *continue* supporting cuts in federal programs when you have the option of living in a community where very few people have an income lower than your own and where you can receive adequate local services without paying too much in local taxes. According to this argument, suburbanization serves as an important link in sustaining and perpetuating existing political preferences because it fundamentally affects the calculus of self-interest.

Consequently, this contextual argument is somewhat different from some other contemporary discussions of contextual effects—for example, claims about the effects of living in areas of extreme, concentrated poverty on the likelihood of dropping out of school or becoming a teenage parent.[19] The notion that living in a suburb affects political attitudes is not an argument about the direct effect of environment on behavior but rather an argument that the type of community in which an individual lives may provide him or her with a particular set of interests in addition to those interests generated by individual-level characteristics. As discussed in chapter 2, this mechanism is suggested by Abbott in his discussion of Sun Belt cities: "When most residents of the [suburb] have no contact, no concern, and no interest in the old core neighborhoods, suburbanites will tend to direct their political life without particular reference to the central city."[20]

Another example of the way in which geography alters self-interest—and creates resultant policy consequences—is provided by Massey and Denton in their study of segregation. They argue that even in the absence of racial prejudice, "segregation undermines the ability of blacks to advance their interests because it provides ethnic whites with no immediate self-interest in [blacks'] welfare."[21] In other words, our political self-interest is not defined solely by our individual-level characteristics but also by the characteristics of our environment.

Notes

1. The following statistical techniques were employed: ordinary least squares analysis with dependent variables that take more than four values, logit analysis with dichotomous dependent variables, and ordered probit analysis with dependent variables that take three or four values.

2. The models were also run with ideology instead of party identification as an independent variable, yielding results that were not substantially different.

3. Living in a suburb and religious affiliation were significantly correlated during the 1950s, with Protestants more likely to live in the suburbs and Jews more likely to live in the city. For the contemporary period, the possibility of an important connection between suburban politics and the politics of the religious right was also considered. Consequently, the Protestant variable was broken down to distinguish born-again Protestants from others in the analysis. However, the inclusion of this distinction did not affect the models of vote choice or party identification during the 1988–1992 period.

4. This variable was available only for 1992.

5. An alternative hypothesis is suggested by Zikmund, who argues that the nationwide division between urban and suburban voters is not very significant because urban and suburban residents of the same metropolitan area tend to be united around common concerns: "all parts of a particular metropolitan area share common problems and a common political, social, and economic environment." In Zikmund's view, suburban residents who are concerned about the blight they see in their neighboring city may be no less supportive of aid to cities than urban residents. See Joseph Zikmund II, "A Comparison of Political Attitude and Activity Patterns in Central Cities and Suburbs," *Public Opinion Quarterly* 31, no. 1 (spring 1967):75.

6. William Schneider, "The Suburban Century Begins: The Real Meaning of the 1992 Election," *Atlantic Monthly*, July 1992.

7. Thomas Byrne Edsall and Mary D. Edsall, *Chain Reaction: The Impact of Race, Rights, and Taxes on American Politics* (New York: W.W. Norton, 1992), 228.

8. Even this methodology is not necessarily foolproof. As studies of participants in the Gautreaux program illustrate, questions may still remain about the degree to which those who decide to move are comparable to those with similar demographic characteristics who do not decide to move.

9. Calculated from data in table 18, "Geographic Mobility, Commuting, and Veteran Status, 1990," in Bureau of the Census, *1990 Census of Population. Social and Economic Characteristics* (Washington, D.C.: GPO, November 1992).

10. Ralph R. Sell, "Analyzing Migration Decisions: The First Step—Whose Decisions?" *Demography* 20, no. 3 (August 1983).

11. Ibid.

12. William H. Frey and Alden Speare Jr., *Regional and Metropolitan Growth and Decline in the United States* (New York: Russell Sage Foundation, 1988). See also Charles Tiebout, "A Pure Theory of Local Expenditures," *Journal of Political Economy* 64, no. 5 (October 1956).

13. Frederick M. Wirt et al., *On the City's Rim: Politics and Policy in Suburbia* (Lexington, Mass.: D.C. Heath, 1972), 129–30.

14. Evan McKenzie, *Privatopia: Homeowner Associations and the Rise of Residential Private Government* (New Haven, Conn.: Yale University Press, 1994), 105.

15. Ibid., 11–12.

16. The *Newsweek* poll was cited in Renee Loth, "Citifying Suburbia: It Isn't What It Was, US Census Figures Show," *Boston Globe*, 3 November 1991, p. B17. The *New York Times* survey results appeared in Elizabeth Kolbert, "Region around New York Sees Ties to City Faltering," *New York Times*, 1 December 1991, p. A1, and in William Glaberson, "For Many in the New York Region, the City Is Ignored and Irrelevant," *New York Times*, 2 January 1992, p. A1.

17. This argument will be explored in more depth in chapter 7, which discusses the consequences of an increasingly suburban electorate for congressional politics.

18. Robert Huckfeldt, "Ethnic Politics," *American Politics Quarterly* 11, no. 1 (January 1983), 117.

19. See William Julius Wilson, *The Truly Disadvantaged: The Inner City, the Underclass, and Public Policy* (Chicago: University of Chicago Press, 1987). For a discussion of neighborhood effects, see Christopher Jencks and Susan E. Mayer, "The Social Consequences of Growing Up in a Poor Neighborhood," in *Inner-City Poverty in the United States,* ed. Laurence E. Lynn Jr. and Michael G. H. McGeary (Washington, D.C.: National Academy Press, 1990).

20. Carl Abbott, *The New Urban America: Growth and Politics in Sunbelt Cities* (Chapel Hill: University of North Carolina Press, 1987), 213.

21. Douglas S. Massey and Nancy A. Denton, *American Apartheid: Segregation and the Making of the Underclass* (Cambridge, Mass.: Harvard University Press, 1993), 160.

CHAPTER FIVE

Party Identification, Vote Choice, and Policy Preferences in the Suburbs

Suburban Politics, 1952–1992

Many contemporary observers of the suburbs have suggested that the late 1980s and early 1990s represented a unique point in American history when particular political and economic forces combined to create a geography-based politics. As an increasingly insecure middle class turned its back on the rest of America, insulating itself within the boundaries of closely controlled communities, suburbia became home to a majority of voters, and support for national solutions to national problems declined.[1] But notions of the political significance of suburban living are hardly new. While many of these earlier discussions were more sociological than political, Robert Wood argued as early as the 1950s that the real significance of the suburbs was the privatization of resources and the refusal to bear the cost of solutions to problems that existed outside the boundary of the local community.[2]

The first portion of this chapter, which examines historical data on vote choice and party identification for the years 1952 to 1992, directly addresses previous studies of suburbanization by comparing the results for earlier decades with those for the late 1980s and 1990s.

Is the contemporary period unique? Were earlier studies of suburban political behavior correct in concluding that the assumed relationship between suburbanization and particular political attitudes did not exist during the 1950s, 1960s, and 1970s? The second portion of the chapter turns from these questions to a more in-depth analysis of data from the contemporary period—1988 to 1992.

Earlier political scientists reached consensus that the empirical evidence failed to support the claims of a distinctive suburban politics, but they were limited by the available data and statistical methods. For example, because most of the early work relied on community-level rather than on individual-level data, behavior that was observed only in the aggregate was attributed to individuals.[3] Thus, it was not the behavior of suburban individuals but that of suburban communities that was explored; moreover, characteristics that may have explained political preferences—other than where people live—were not controlled for.[4]

Methodology

The analysis presented here relies on National Election Study (NES) data from 1952 to 1992 to explore the influence of suburban living over time. Because it was difficult to find questions that had been asked in substantially the same form for every year of the study, the choice of dependent variables was limited to party identification, congressional vote choice, and presidential vote choice. While these variables do not completely capture the range of arguments made today about the political relevance of suburbs, they are the very same variables used in most earlier studies of the effects of suburban living. Thus, they are useful as a point of comparison with earlier studies.

The previous chapter laid out the choice of independent variables in detail, so only a few will be mentioned here that are specific to the historical analysis. In addition to controls for the year of the study, the suburban variable (coded 1 for living in a suburb and 0 for living in a central city) was included on its own and was used to create dummy variables for each time period of the analysis. Control variables for homeownership and for being married with children were not included, since this information was not available for all years of the National Election Studies.

Results: Rise of a Distinctive Politics

The results of the analysis lend credence to the hypothesis that living in a suburb is associated with a distinctive politics and that this association is a relatively new development. During the entire forty-year period, living in a suburb was significantly associated with supporting the Republican Party and Republican congressional candidates. However, when the findings were broken down by time period, living in a suburb achieved statistical significance only between 1988 and 1992. Suburban living may have been related to political behavior in earlier decades, but during the late 1980s and early 1990s the strength and size of the relationship increased substantially (tables 7, 8, and 9).[5] Similarly, the model for presidential vote choice shows that only during the 1980s was living in a suburb consistently associated with an increased probability of voting Republican. Living in a suburb was not significantly related to presidential vote choice during the 1960s or 1970s, nor was the overall suburban variable significant (tables 10 and 11). The next three sections take a more detailed look at these results.

Party Identification

Living in a suburb was significantly related to an increased likelihood of identifying as a Republican during the entire time period. This effect was moderate: a movement of just under one-fourth of a point on a seven-point identification scale. A movement of one-fourth of a point would mean, for example, a shift one-quarter of the way from being a strong Republican to being a weak Republican or from being a weak Democrat to being an Independent who leans toward the Democratic Party. Another way to gain a sense of the size of the relationship between living in a suburb and identifying as a Republican is to compare it to the size of the relationship between party identification and other variables. For example, it is slightly less than one-fifth the size of the racial effect and is equivalent in size to a two-point movement on the income scale (see table 7).

When the time period is broken down into smaller increments, however, the relationship between party identification and suburban living approaches significance only during the 1988–1992 period. The size of the effect for these years is almost double that of earlier time periods. With all else held constant, living in a suburb between 1952 and 1992 is associated with a movement of almost one-fourth of a point in the Republican direction, but living in a suburb between 1988 and 1992 is associated with a movement of more than two-fifths of a point in the Republican direction.

Yet another way to understand the relationship between living in a suburb and party identification in the 1988–1992 period is to observe how the expected value of a hypothetical person's party identification changes when all characteristics except location are held constant. A white Catholic female who is between forty-five and fifty-four years of age, who has some college and a family income in the 34th to 67th percentile, and who lives in a non-Southern city has an expected party identification score of 3.38. This classifies her as an Independent who leans toward the Democratic Party. The same person living in the suburbs has an expected score of 3.80, which brings her closer to being classified as a pure Independent.

Congressional Vote Choice

Living in a suburb was significantly associated with an increased likelihood of voting for a Republican member of Congress during the entire time period. However, during the 1988–1992 time period, the suburban coefficient was more than twice that for the time period overall (see table 8). As with party identification, while living in a suburb appears to have had political significance before the late 1980s, the relationship clearly strengthened during the contemporary period.

Holding all characteristics constant except location, the same hypothetical white female Catholic described earlier has a 24 percent probability of voting for a Republican member of Congress if she lives in the city and a 39 percent probability if she lives in a suburb.

As discussed in chapter 4, models of vote choice that treated party identification as an independent variable were also used. As expected, the inclusion of party identification takes explanatory power away from the other variables: the general "living-in-a-suburb" variable no longer achieves statistical significance. Nevertheless, living in a suburb remained significant for the 1988–1992 period, although the size of the relationship was reduced somewhat, from a coefficient of 0.50 to a coefficient of 0.40 (see table 9). Again, this finding suggests that the relationship between suburban living and political behavior was stronger in the 1988–1992 time period than in the fifties, sixties, seventies, or early eighties.

Presidential Vote Choice

Living in a suburb was significantly related to presidential vote choice only in the 1980–1986 period (see table 10). During that same time period, living in a suburb remained significantly related to presidential vote choice even with the inclusion of party identification as an explanatory variable (see table 11). Holding everything constant except the location of the respondent, the same white Catholic female described previously had a 40 percent probability of voting for a Republican if she lived in the city but a 56 percent probability if she lived in the suburbs.

The Timing of the Suburban Political Era

The findings support the argument that the rise of a distinctive suburban politics is a relatively recent occurrence. While during earlier decades living in a suburb was sometimes significantly associated with a propensity to identify as a Republican or to vote for Republican congressional and presidential candidates, since 1980 that relationship has clearly been stronger and more consistent. These findings make sense in the context of the arguments in chapter 2 that the late 1980s and early 1990s represented a period when suburbanites were increasingly able to separate from the cities and when cities increasingly gave them reason to want to separate.

In contrast to the findings for party identification and congressional vote are the findings for presidential vote. The relationship between living in a suburb during the 1988–1992 period and the expected presidential vote is relatively weak, while the relationship is strongest during the first half of the 1980s. However, if one considers the elections involved, this difference is not as troubling as it might at first appear. Ronald Reagan's two elections occurred in the first half of the 1980s, and the findings here support the idea that those who crossed Democratic Party lines to vote for Reagan were to a large extent from the suburbs. In addition, the 1992 election, which is encompassed in the most recent time period discussed, included the candidacy of Ross Perot—which, many observers argued, drew suburban support away from the Republican candidate. (The analysis of the Perot vote that follows will show this to be the case.) Furthermore, these findings suggest that Clinton's victory in 1992 was not necessarily about gaining a suburban advantage but rather about mitigating the suburban advantage of the Republican Party.

Suburban Politics, 1988–1992

In this section, the findings for the contemporary period will be used as background for a more detailed analysis of the data. Because there was greater consistency in the questions asked across surveys during this narrower time span, it was possible to expand the number of dependent variables—which, in turn, allowed a more nuanced exploration of the political implications of suburbanization.[6]

Results: The Political Preferences of Suburbanites

The two arguments generally made about the inhabitants of suburbs are that, on the one hand, suburbs are so different from each other that generalizations about suburbs and suburbanites are meaningless; and on the other hand, that a distinctive suburban politics is no more than the politics of the white middle class. A look at the survey respondents provides evidence for both arguments: suburbanites are clearly not homogeneous, and they do, in the aggregate, differ in several ways from city residents (table 12).

Although the suburban and city samples are similar with respect to gender distribution, level of education, and mean age, suburban residents are more likely to be white and to fall at the higher end of the income distribution scale. While 90 percent of the suburban sample is white, only 70 percent of the urban sample is white. The incomes of 24 percent of suburbanites are at or below the 33rd percentile, while 35 percent of urban residents fall into this income range. Similarly, 76 percent of suburban residents have incomes in the 34th to 100th percentile, while only 65 percent of urban residents fall into this range. Multivariate analysis makes it possible to determine whether city-suburban political differences are a consequence of these demographic differences or exist independently of them.

Vote Choice

In keeping with recent media reports, suburban voters did display stronger support than city voters for the Republican presidential candidate in the 1988 and 1992 elections. The Republicans received 52.0 percent of the suburban vote but only 32.4 percent of the urban vote. Despite arguments about the pivotal role of the suburban vote, once variables like age, race, and party identification are controlled for, location had no significant independent effect on whether respondents voted for the Republican or Democratic presidential candidate during the 1988–1992 period (table 13). However, when party identification is omitted as an independent variable, living in a suburb does increase the probability of supporting the Republican presidential candidate (table 14).

This significant finding is in contrast to the findings that were derived from the cumulative data. But it does not change the fact that the relationship between presidential vote and living in a suburb was stronger in the early 1980s than in the late 1980s and early 1990s. The earlier discussion of the cumulative data suggested that the weakness of the relationship between location and presidential vote was caused by the fact that the 1992 suburban vote was drawn away from the Republican candidate toward the Independent candidate Ross Perot. Findings based on the 1992 NES data lend support to this hypothesis (table 15).

Location was a significant variable in explaining the vote for Perot. While party identification was of little use in explaining a vote for Perot, age and education were negatively and significantly related to voting for Perot, and income was positively related, as was being white and being male. However, even after these variables were controlled for, living in a suburb increased the probability of a vote for Perot. Moreover, living in a suburb remained significant even when homeownership and being married with children were included in the model.

Holding all variables except location constant and noting the changes in the probability of voting for Perot illustrates the effect of living in a suburb. For example, a single, thirty-year-old African American male Protestant with some college, whose income is in the 34th to 67th percentile, who does not own a home, who identifies as a weak Democrat, and who lives in a non-Southern city has a 12 percent probability of voting for Perot. In the suburbs, this same individual has an 18 percent probability of voting for Perot.

Since voters may use different criteria to select congressional candidates than they use to select presidential candidates, the relationship between location and congressional votes was also explored. Before any socioeconomic characteristics have been controlled for, it is clear that Republican congressional candidates have an advantage in the suburbs: among the NES sample, Republicans received 44 percent of congressional votes in the suburbs but only 24 percent in the city. To see whether these differences remained when socioeconomic differences were taken into account, the congressional vote was regressed on location, socioeconomic variables, party identification, and incumbency. Once party identification and incumbency had been taken into account, few other variables remained statistically significant.

However, living in a suburb did significantly increase the probability of voting for the Republican candidate, even with controls for these other variables (table 16), and this effect remained even after homeownership and being married with children were controlled for: neither of these variables was significantly related to congressional vote. Controls for incumbency were also included in this model: two dummy variables, one for the presence of a Democratic incumbent and one for the presence of a Republican incumbent. The significant effect of living in a suburb can perhaps be explained by the fact that the incumbent in a suburban area is more likely to be a Republican (and therefore a suburbanite voting for the incumbent is more likely to be voting for a Republican). Nevertheless, although both the incumbency variables are statistically significant, the location variable remains significant even when they are included.

Once again, a hypothetical example of the effect of living in a suburb is illustrative. A married, forty-five-year-old white female with some college education and an income in the 34th to 67th percentile who owns a home, identifies as a weak Democrat, and lives in a non-Southern city in a district with a Republican incumbent has a 46 percent probability of voting for the Republican congressional candidate. This same individual in the suburbs has a 56 percent probability of voting for the Republican congressional candidate.

While this increased probability is the direct relationship between living in a suburb and congressional vote, the actual size of the relationship may be even larger, given that part of the effect of location may work indirectly through party identification. To test this proposition, party identification was regressed on the control variables, which revealed that living in a suburb had a significant effect on party identification even when socioeconomic factors were controlled for (table 17).

With all other variables held constant, living in a suburb is associated with a movement of slightly less than one-half of a point in the Republican direction on a seven-point scale. This may not seem like a strong association, but a comparison with other variables provides context: for example, the relationship between gender and party identification is less than half the size.

This finding for party identification suggests that an indirect effect of living in a suburb works through party identification, and that there may therefore be an even stronger relationship between living in a suburb and congressional vote. Despite this finding, it is primarily the results of models that include party identification as a control variable that will be reported, since the inclusion of party identification creates a higher hurdle for the suburb variable and should offer a more persuasive argument to skeptics. However, if one accepts the argument that the causal link between living in a suburb and party identification may run at least partially from the former to the latter, then the size of the relationship between suburban living and political attitudes may be even larger than reported.

Federal Spending

The findings show that even after individual-level variables are controlled for, suburban residents are more likely than city residents to support cutting federal aid to cities (table 18). Identifying as a Republican, being younger, and being white are all significantly related to a preference for cutting aid to cities. In addition, homeownership and being married with children are significantly related to an increased probability of favoring less aid. The inclusion of these two variables, however, does not negate the impact of location.

Again, an example can offer some perspective on the extent of the relationship. A forty-five-year-old African American male with mean income and education who identifies as a weak Democrat and lives in the city has a 33 percent probability of supporting decreased spending on cities. This same individual in the suburbs has a 38 percent probability of supporting decreased spending on cities.

Living in a suburb also has a significant relationship to opinion about spending on programs that assist blacks (table 19). If all other variables are held constant, a forty-five-year-old white female who has some college education, an income in the 34th to 67th percentile, and lives in a non-Southern city has a 22 percent probability of supporting decreased spending on programs to assist blacks. However, if she lives in the suburbs, she has a 25 percent probability of supporting decreased spending on such programs. The effect of living in a suburb on spending programs, while significant, is not huge. However, there is again the possibility that an indirect effect of living in a suburb may work through the party identification variable. The size of the coefficient increases by one-third when party identification is not included as a control variable (to –0.21, with a standard error of 0.05).

Location is also significantly related to responses to a general question about government spending and service provision (table 20). With all other variables held constant, living in a suburb, as opposed to a city, is associated with a 0.18-point decrease on a seven-point scale. An indirect effect operating through party identification can again be taken into account: the coefficient when party identification is excluded is -0.26, with a standard error of 0.07.

Once socioeconomic variables and party identification are controlled for, the effect of living in a suburb on opinion about spending on food stamps falls short of statistical significance (table 21). However, when party identification is excluded as a control variable, the effect of living in a suburb is again significant (table 22).

Responses to the feeling thermometer question, which measured how close respondents felt to welfare recipients, varied by location, with 54.8 percent of city residents—compared with only 44.6 percent of suburban residents—placing themselves at 60 degrees or above. Once socioeconomic variables are introduced, party identification, age, income, race, and being a homeowner are significantly related to scores on the feeling thermometer. However, the significance of location did not disappear (table 23). With all other variables held constant, living in a suburb as opposed to a city is associated with a drop on the feeling thermometer of 2.2 degrees.

Responses to spending on Social Security also differed by location. Very few people in either cities or suburbs wanted to cut spending on Social Security (3.3 and 3.7 percent, respectively). However, more suburban residents wanted to keep spending the same (42.1 percent, compared with 35.2 percent), and more city residents wanted to increase spending (61.5 percent, compared with 54.3 percent). When location was included in a model with socioeconomic variables, however, the significance of living in a suburb disappeared: party identification, age, income, education, gender, race, and being married with children were all significant (table 24). This time, excluding party identification did not affect the significance of location.

The Suburban Voter: Expectations versus Reality

The results suggest that suburbanites do have a distinctive politics, although not always along the lines described in contemporary discussions of suburbia. Once socioeconomic differences are accounted for, suburbanites are still more opposed to government spending than their urban counterparts. The finding that suburbanites are less supportive of spending on cities, food stamps, and programs that assist blacks supports the idea that suburbanites are generally opposed to governmental aid. However, the finding that location is not significantly related to attitudes toward spending on Social Security suggests that this opposition is not as pronounced when the beneficiaries are primarily those in the middle class.

On the other hand, the significant finding on the question about government spending and services in general may suggest that suburbanites are not only opposed to spending on the poor but are more likely than urban dwellers to oppose all government spending. This interpretation of the finding depends, however, on what kinds of spending and programs the respondents imagined when the question was asked. Edsall and Edsall argue that suburbanites increasingly associate government spending and services with the idea of taking money from the middle class to help the undeserving poor.[7] It is quite probable that respondents would have interpreted a general question about government spending as a question about spending on redistributive programs rather than as a question about middle-class benefits like Social Security. Therefore, the question received responses that were similar to those for the questions on specific spending programs.

The finding that suburbanites were more likely to vote for Perot is in keeping with much that was written about the Perot vote in 1992. However, it is somewhat surprising that the increased likelihood of voting for Perot remains even after socioeconomic variables are controlled for. Again, this finding seems to point toward a stronger anti-government feeling in the suburbs than in the cities. In addition, it may help to explain the weakening of the relationship between living in a suburb and presidential vote choice during the 1988–1992 period. While suburbanites voted disproportionately for Reagan in 1980 and 1984, they turned away from the two parties and toward Perot in 1992. In the 1996 presidential election, the need to attract suburban voters seemed once again to be an important component of the two main candidates' campaign strategies. Clinton and Dole's courting of the "suburban mom" vote helps to explain why increasing suburbanization did not lead, as earlier suburban scholars had predicted, to Republican political dominance. In a two-party system, both parties will move toward the center—and in the 1980s and 1990s, the center was increasingly suburban. (The partisan response to suburbanization will be explored in greater detail in chapter 8.)

Even more surprising than the significant finding for the Perot vote once control variables are taken into account is the significant finding for congressional vote choice. The initial explanation for this finding was that the incumbent in a suburban area is more likely to be a Republican—and a suburbanite voting for an incumbent is therefore more likely to be voting for a Republican. However, even with the inclusion of two dummy variables for the presence of a Democratic or Republican incumbent, living in a suburb remained significantly related to congressional vote choice.

These significant findings—the role of location in congressional vote choice and the fact that suburbanites are more likely to identify as Republicans even after socioeconomic characteristics are taken into account—are particularly surprising because they are exactly the findings that researchers in the 1960s and 1970s expected to uncover and did not. Does this mean that, as was suggested in the 1950s, a move to the suburbs means a move toward the Republican Party? Probably not, but it does suggest that the Republican Party was, in the late 1980s and early 1990s, doing a better job of giving voice to the distinctive concerns of suburbanites.[8] The way in which the suburbanization of American politics has affected congressional and presidential politics will be explored in greater detail in chapters 7 and 8.

How significant are these results? In keeping with contemporary discussions of suburbia—and in opposition to earlier research—the analysis does offer evidence of a distinctive suburban political behavior that is not accounted for by differences in socioeconomic characteristics. As was discussed in the previous chapter, it is not possible at the moment to assert causality: are suburban voters distinctive because they live in the suburbs, or do they move to the suburbs because they are distinctive? Probably the answer is a combination of the two: particular kinds of people leave the city for the suburbs—and, once they are there, certain of their behaviors and attitudes are reinforced. However, it should be noted that, in general, this relationship between location and politics persists not only when socioeconomic characteristics are controlled for but also when party identification is taken into account. If preexisting political attitudes are causally related to the move to the suburbs, then one might expect the inclusion of party identification to eliminate the suburban effect.

The finding that location affects politics even when socioeconomic variables and party identification are controlled for raises an important question: What distinctive features of suburbanites lead to their distinctive politics? This analysis tested two suburban features that had possible political relevance: homeownership and being married with children, independent variables that were sometimes statistically significant. In particular, homeownership was consistently associated with decreased support for spending on government programs. However, this finding appeared to be unrelated to living in a suburb: that is, the inclusion of homeownership did not affect the statistical significance of the suburban variable.

It may be, then, that what is important about being suburban has less to do with the characteristics of a particular person than with the characteristics of the people who surround that person. For example, what matters is not that an individual owns a home but that he lives in area where most of the residents also own their homes. This explanation would be in keeping with the argument that, as some have suggested, the most important characteristic of suburbia is the ability to meet local spending and service needs without going outside local boundaries. Ultimately, specific features of suburbia may be important only to the extent that they contribute to the ability or the desire of suburbanites to insulate themselves from demands originating outside the local community. The relationship between political attitudes and specific features of suburban areas that contribute to both the desire and the ability to be insulated from the city will be explored in chapter 6, in which National Election Study data and census data are combined to create a more differentiated understanding of suburbia.

The use of census data will also help to address another issue raised by the findings described in this chapter. The relationships between suburban residence and distinctive behaviors and attitudes, while significant, are not large. However, because these findings are derived from analyses that made no attempt to differentiate between kinds of suburbs—small and large, old and new were all classified identically—the finding of even a relatively small effect is interesting. If suburbs are broken down according to characteristics like population size, age, and socioeconomic and racial composition, particular kinds of suburbs may be even more strongly associated with a distinctive kind of politics. An investigation of this possibility is the focus of chapter 6.

Notes

1. William Schneider, "The Suburban Century Begins: The Real Meaning of the 1992 Election," *Atlantic Monthly*, July 1992; Katherine S. Newman, *Declining Fortunes: The Withering of the American Dream* (New York: Basic Books, 1993); Thomas Byrne Edsall and Mary D. Edsall, *Chain Reaction: The Impact of Race, Rights, and Taxes on American Politics* (New York: W.W. Norton, 1992); Robert B. Reich, *Tales of a New America* (New York: Times Books, 1987); Mike Davis, *City of Quartz: Excavating the Future in Los Angeles* (New York: Vintage Books, 1990).

2. Robert C. Wood, *Suburbia: Its People and Their Politics* (Boston: Houghton Mifflin, 1958).

3. Joseph Zikmund II, "A Comparison of Political Attitude and Activity Patterns in Central Cities and Suburbs," *Public Opinion Quarterly* 31, no. 1 (spring 1967); Zikmund, "Suburban Voting in Presidential Elections," *Midwest Journal of Political Science* 12, no. 2 (May 1968); Herbert Hirsch, "Suburban Voting and National Trends: A Research Note," *Western Political Quarterly* 21, no. 3 (September 1968).

4. *On the City's Rim*, by Frederick M. Wirt et al., one of the most comprehensive explorations of suburban political behavior, does analyze individual-level data, but only for the year 1968, and the results are somewhat hard to interpret because the coefficients and standard errors are not reported. See *On the City's Rim: Politics and Policy in Suburbia* (Lexington, Mass.: D.C. Heath, 1972).

5. This analysis was also performed with the data from the 1950s, 1960s, and 1970s broken down into smaller spans of years—as was done for the data from the late 1980s and early 1990s—with substantially the same results: living in a suburb was not significantly related to vote choice or party identification during these earlier time periods.

6. The selection of these dependent variables and their relationship to current arguments about suburban political behavior were discussed in detail in the preceding chapter.

7. Edsall and Edsall, *Chain Reaction*.

8. This is exactly the argument that Edsall and Edsall make in *Chain Reaction*.

CHAPTER SIX

Suburban Diversity and
Metropolitan Context

Chapter 5 offered evidence for the existence of important city-suburb differences in political attitudes and behaviors—differences that remain even after individual-level socioeconomic characteristics are taken into account. These results are interesting for two reasons: first, because they are contrary to the findings of earlier research, which found that living in a suburb had little independent effect on the politics of residents; and second, because they are instead in accord with current popular notions of how suburbanization affects national politics.[1]

However, these findings leave a number of important questions unanswered. First, while the relationship between suburban living and distinctive political attitudes is consistent, it is usually fairly small. What happens to this relationship if distinctions are made between particular kinds of suburbs in particular kinds of metropolitan areas? Second, one of the most common criticisms of discussions of suburbia is that the term *suburb* encompasses such diverse locations as to be almost meaningless. While the analysis so far shows that the distinction between city and suburb remains meaningful even without distinguishing between types of suburban areas, what happens to city-suburb differences when the diversity of suburban areas is taken into account?

The analysis in this chapter is based on two distinct, but not incompatible, hypotheses about the effect of differentiating between types of suburbs. One observation sometimes made about suburbs is that as they age, they come to resemble cities and to experience more of the problems traditionally associated with cities.[2] Therefore, the first hypothesis was that residents of suburban areas with "citylike" features would diverge less in attitudes and behaviors from city residents than would residents of more "traditional" suburbs. Another important contemporary perspective is that suburbanization represents a retreat from the problems found in cities.[3] Thus, the second hypothesis was that metropolitan context would affect the difference in attitudes between suburban and city residents: if suburban residents are indeed reacting against the problems that they see in cities, then a distinctive suburban politics should be most clearly exhibited in those areas where the city is particularly unattractive or where the differences between the city and surrounding suburbs are particularly great.[4]

It is entirely plausible that residents living in suburban areas that have more citylike characteristics differ less from city dwellers than do other suburbanites *and* that the differences between suburban and city residents are conditioned by the metropolitan environment that they inhabit. While it might be interesting to be able to distinguish the findings for each hypothesis by including all the independent variables describing location in one model, the limitations of the data do not permit this. Consequently, each hypothesis will be tested and discussed separately.

Suburban Variation

In the analysis, the three characteristics used to differentiate suburban areas are population change, percentage of the population living in poverty, and percentage of the population that is black. It should be noted that these variables describe suburban rings rather than individual suburbs. This choice substantially simplifies the task at hand, but it also means that a significant amount of suburban diversity—that occurring within a metropolitan area—may be obscured. However, characteristics of the suburban ring do give an overall sense of the character of the suburbs and how they vary across metropolitan areas. Suburbs with declining populations, relatively high levels of poor residents, and relatively large African American populations resemble cities more than they resemble the typical image of white middle-class suburbia. Therefore, one would expect these characteristics to be associated with a reduction in the divergence between the political attitudes of suburban and city residents.

There are many reasons to expect these characteristics that make suburbs more like cities to be positively correlated with one another. Although black suburbanization has been an important phenomenon in the past two decades and does represent the rise of an African American middle class, analysis of census data shows that suburbs with higher percentages of black residents tend to experience more citylike problems than those with smaller percentages of black residents.[5] In addition, population decline has been shown to correspond to high levels of poverty and to the presence of a large black population.[6]

As table 25—which shows the correlation coefficients for these three variables—reveals, the percentage of the population that is black and the percentage living in poverty are positively correlated. While population decline is only weakly correlated with the percentage of the population living in poverty, it is more strongly correlated with the percentage of the population that is black. This finding is in keeping with the results presented by Bradbury, Downs, and Small in *Urban Decline and the Future of American Cities* and with those of Massey and Denton in *American Apartheid*. Both books argue that the white exodus from cities was preceded not by an increase in urban poverty but by changes in the racial composition of urban areas.

Methodology

To test the relationship between the attitudes of suburban residents and the characteristics of the suburban rings in which they live, it was necessary to match census data to the location variables contained in the National Election Studies. The census data was used to distinguish between suburban rings; these different suburban areas were then compared with cities in general. The poverty and race variables were expressed as percentages for the suburban ring in each metro area, while population decline was expressed as a dichotomous variable coded 1 if the suburban ring lost population between 1980 and 1990 and 0 if it gained population. Table 26, which shows how the suburban rings within each metropolitan area differed along these three dimensions, offers a glimpse of the range of variation among the suburban areas that were included in the NES sample.

An interaction term was then created between each of the measures of suburban diversity and the dichotomous living-in-a-suburb variable. Both these new interaction terms and the original dichotomous suburb variable were then included in the same models of vote choice and opinion that were discussed in chapter 4 and used in chapter 5.[7]

The original suburban variable was included in order to determine whether the general gap between city and suburban respondents was smaller or larger for respondents in particular kinds of suburbs. The usual socioeconomic control variables were also included: age, income, education, gender, race, religion, living in the South, homeownership, and being married with children.[8]

Suburban Politics: Variation across Suburban Areas

The findings generally supported the hypothesis that residents of citylike suburban areas would differ less from city residents than would residents of more traditional suburban areas. As can be seen from the last four rows in tables 27, 28, and 29, taking the smaller positive coefficients for the differentiated suburban variables into account reduces the large negative coefficient for the dichotomous living-in-a-suburb variable.

Residents of suburban rings with higher percentages of black residents and residents of suburban rings that are losing population are more supportive of the Democratic Party in general than other suburban residents, although not more supportive than city residents. Residents of suburban rings with higher percentages of black residents are also more supportive of Democratic candidates for Congress and for president than other suburban residents—or at least not as supportive of Republican candidates. The poverty rate of the suburban area, however, has no significant relationship to any of the dependent variables once the other two location variables are controlled for.

Because the interaction between the dichotomous and differentiated suburban variables makes the results somewhat difficult to interpret from tables 27, 28, and 29, tables 30 and 31 give examples of hypothetical individuals and show how their vote choice and political attitudes are expected to vary in different suburban contexts.

As table 30 illustrates, controlling for population decline and for the size of the black population increases the divergence in predicted vote choice for city and suburban residents: a thirty-five-year-old white Protestant woman who owns a home, is married with children, and has mean education and income has a 44 percent probability of voting for the Republican presidential candidate if she lives in a city, but a 70 percent probability if she lives in a non-declining suburb with almost no black population. Similarly, in a congressional district without an incumbent, this woman has a 46 percent probability of voting for a Republican candidate for Congress if she lives in the city but a 77 percent probability if she lives in a growing suburban area with no black population.

As expected, such differences between city and suburban residents decrease if the suburbs have more citylike characteristics. For example, in a suburban area that has a 12 percent black population, this same woman has a 53 percent probability of voting for the Republican presidential candidate, as opposed to a 44 percent probability if she lived in a city and 70 percent if she lived in a homogeneous suburban area. Similarly, in an area with a 12 percent black population, she has a 47 percent probability of voting for the Republican candidate for Congress, compared with 46 percent if she lived in a city and 77 percent if she lived in a homogeneous suburban area.

The substantive significance of the effect on party identification is less clear because a one-half- to three-quarter-point move on the seven-point identification scale is difficult to translate into meaningful change in party identification. A three-quarter-point shift would almost be enough to move a respondent from a strong Democrat to a weak Democrat, while a one-half-point move would leave the respondent somewhere between the two.

A comparison with some of the other explanatory variables may be useful. For example, women are generally thought to favor the Democratic Party. In this analysis, with all else held constant, being a woman shifted respondents just under one-fifth of a point in the Democratic direction—less than living in a suburb. On the other hand, being black shifted respondents more than one whole point: from "leaning Democratic" toward "strong Democrat," for example. What is clear about party identification is that the general pattern is consistent: the largest city-suburb difference occurs when the suburban area in question is mainly white and not declining in population. When the size of the African American population increases or the suburban area begins to experience population decline, the divergence between the partisan identification of city and suburban residents begins to decrease.

The effect of a higher percentage of black residents on two other dependent variables—support for spending on programs to assist blacks and scores on the feeling thermometer, which measured how close respondents felt to welfare recipients—was much the same as it had been on suburban vote probabilities. As table 28 illustrates, when the black population of the suburban area increases, the city-suburb differences in support for spending and in scores on the feeling thermometer both decrease. However, in striking contrast to the results for vote choice, living in a suburban area that is experiencing population decline increases the divergence between city and suburban residents on two measures: support for spending on programs to assist blacks and scores on the feeling thermometer question.

To understand the effect of a change in location on the probability of supporting a decrease in spending on programs to assist blacks, it is useful to compare changes in probabilities when everything but location is held constant. As shown in table 31, a fifty-year-old white Jewish man who owns a home, is married with children, and has mean education and income has a 25 percent probability of supporting decreased spending on programs to assist blacks if he lives in a city, but a 37 percent probability if he lives in a suburban ring that is experiencing population decline but has almost no black population. On the other hand, if he lives in a suburban ring that is not experiencing population decline but that has a 12 percent black population, he has a 27 percent probability of supporting decreased spending—a probability that is close to that for a city dweller. The fitted values for the feeling thermometer responses show the same relationships: the expected scores for the same man range from 54 (out of 100) if he lives in the city to 45 if he lives in a suburban area that is experiencing population decline but has almost no black residents.

For the other remaining dependent variables—spending on food stamps, spending on Social Security, and general government spending and services—differentiating between types of suburbs affects only the expected impact of location on respondents' attitudes toward general government spending. If all else is held constant, living in a suburb is associated with a drop in support for government spending and services of more than one-third of a point (on a seven-point scale). However, this difference shrinks to just over one-quarter of a point when the suburban ring has a 12 percent black population. For spending on food stamps, only the dichotomous suburban variable is significantly associated with less support for spending—and, as was found in chapter 5, the Social Security variable is unaffected by the inclusion of a suburban explanatory variable.

This analysis has shown that, as expected, residents of suburbs with more citylike features are less distinct from city dwellers in their political views than are residents of more traditional suburban areas. With two exceptions, differences in the political attitudes of suburban and city residents remain, but they are smaller than those between city residents and the residents of suburban rings that have more stereo-typically suburban features.

As the percentage of the suburban population that is black increases, the city-suburb gap in the probability that a respondent will vote for the Republican candidate for president or Congress or identify as a Republican begins to decrease. Population decline has a similar relationship to vote choice and party identification. Once the suburbs offer a less secure retreat from the problems of the city, suburban residents seem to become less predictably Republican in their voting.

A larger percentage of black residents is also associated with a decline in the city-suburb gap in support for spending on programs to assist blacks and in scores on the feeling thermometer. While this finding for programs to assist blacks might seem at first unsurprising, it is worth noting that the relationship persists even when the race of the respondent is controlled for: the result is thus more than evidence of simple self-interest. Respondents in suburban areas with higher percentages of black residents may be more likely to see a need for programs to assist blacks than their counterparts in primarily white suburbs either because respondents who live in more racially mixed suburbs have more contact with black residents or because they feel that these programs will ultimately benefit the suburban area in which they live.

For these two dependent variables—spending on programs to assist blacks and attitudes toward welfare recipients—population decline is associated with an increase in city-suburb divergence. Although the reason that decline should operate differently for the attitude variables than for the behavior variables is not immediately clear, it is possible to speculate about the cause.

A look at table 26 reveals that those suburban areas that are experiencing decline are located primarily in the Northeast and the South. It is possible that residents of these regions, while supportive of the Democratic Party generally, are opposed to government spending, which they view as a handout to those other than themselves. (This "other" is invoked explicitly through the questions about programs to assist blacks and through the measurement of attitudes toward welfare recipients.) This explanation is in keeping with the results of post-1988 focus groups that Ed Reilly conducted for the Democratic Party, which are discussed in Edsall and Edsall's *Chain Reaction: The Impact of Race, Rights, and Taxes on American Politics*:

> The race issue, affirmative action, the sense of subsistence programs from the government all going "to people other than myself," to state it politely, is a very prevalent theme with Democrats around the country, especially with those more culturally conservative, northeast Catholics and southern white males. . . . When you get underneath all the code words, the emerging definition of where working class Democrats fit is they talk about themselves as "the people who work."[9]

Residents of suburban areas experiencing population decline may be more Democratic, in terms of vote choice and party identification, than their counterparts in suburban areas where the population is holding steady or growing. But at the same time their experience of population decline and its attendant effects may make them particularly unlikely to support programs that they see as aiding "others"—others whose merit or greater need may, in their view, be in question.

If suburban attitudes change as suburbs begin to resemble cities with respect to racial composition and the percentage of the population living in poverty, then as suburban areas age, the politics of suburban residents may come to resemble those of city dwellers. Such a possibility should give those concerned with the plight of cities cause for optimism, as it suggests a basis for a city-suburb coalition to pressure the federal and state governments to help solve urban problems. At the same time, however, the finding that the experience of population decline increases city-suburban disparities in the level of support for certain programs suggests that this scenario may be unrealistic.

Diminishing support for social programs in the face of population decline can be plausibly interpreted to mean that if a feeling of threat exists, deteriorating suburban conditions may actually make residents even more reluctant to support programs that they view as transferring resources from themselves to others. Even if a suburban area experiences increasingly citylike problems, if the nearby city experiences these problems even more intensely, suburbanites, rather than supporting programs that may result in shared benefit, may be even more unwilling to support federal spending. This hypothesis will be considered in the next section of this chapter.

Metropolitan Variation

Do city dwellers and suburbanites within particular metropolitan contexts differ from each other more or less than their counterparts in other kinds of metropolitan areas? To address this question, it was first necessary to identify ways to differentiate among metropolitan areas, then to develop hypotheses about the relationship between the characteristics of metropolitan areas and the political attitudes of city and suburban dwellers.

Differentiating among Metropolitan Environments

One way to differentiate among metropolitan environments is by region—to compare, for example, city-suburb differences in the West with those in the Northeast. However, because regions are really a proxy for variation in more specific characteristics—the age of the metropolitan area, the number of governments within it, population growth or decline, poverty rate, and racial and ethnic composition—this analysis uses these more specific characteristics to contrast metropolitan environments. To the extent that these characteristics are correlated with region, differences in suburban political preferences in particular kinds of metropolitan areas will also represent differences in suburban political preferences in various regions of the country.

Age of the Metropolitan Area
Age is usually calculated according to the year in which the central city reached a population of 50,000 or more, and this is the

measure that was used here.[10] Metropolitan areas whose cities reached this size by 1900 were grouped together as the oldest areas (coded 7), while the remaining areas were coded in descending order according to how long after 1900 they reached this size. (For example, a metropolitan area whose city reached 50,000 in 1910 was coded 6, 1920 was coded 5, and so on.)

The hypothesis was that suburban residents in older metropolitan areas would display more clearly the distinctive opinions associated with suburban residence in general—in other words, that the difference between city and suburb was likely to be greater. In older metropolitan areas, the city is more likely to have experienced decline and the residents of the surrounding suburbs are more likely to be aware of the costs of tying themselves to the city and its problems. This distinction between new and old metropolitan areas had already been borne out by the analysis of census data included in chapter 3: the metropolitan areas with the smallest differential between the central city and surrounding suburbs on measures like income, unemployment, and homeownership were the newer areas in the southwestern United States.

Growth and Decline

In *Urban Decline and the Future of American Cities,* Bradbury, Downs, and Small note that decline in population is correlated with other measures of decline: increasing poverty and declining income and employment. Thus, one broad measure of urban decline is whether an area is losing or gaining population.[11] On the basis of population patterns for suburbs and cities, four categories of metropolitan area can be defined: those with growing suburbs and growing cities, those with growing suburbs and declining cities, those with declining cities and declining suburbs, and (the smallest category—almost nonexistent) those with growing cities and declining suburbs.

Cities and suburbs were classified as either declining or growing on the basis of population change between 1980 and 1990. The actual measures of population change were then included in the models and coded positive or negative depending on whether the change represented gain or loss.[12]

The hypothesis was that the city-suburb differences in opinion would be greater in an area with a declining central city than in an area with a growing central city. Further, where the contrast between city and suburb was starkest—in areas where the city was declining but the suburban area was growing—the differences were expected to be particularly strong. The reasoning behind this expectation was that instead of motivating suburban residents to "feel the pain" of city dwellers—and support federal programs to address urban problems—the sight of the blighted city would create a "batten-down-the-hatches" mentality.

Expectations for areas in which both city and suburb were declining were less clear. Decline may somewhat reduce the disparity between city and suburban dwellers since both are subject to similar kinds of problems. However, suburban and city residents may still diverge because even declining suburban areas are usually better off than their central city, and the contrast still exists.

Number of Governments

The third variable, the number of governments within the metropolitan area, was based on the number of municipalities. (Townships were classified as municipalities if they assumed most of the functions usually associated with a municipality.) Population size was accounted for by calculating the number of governments per million residents.

The hypothesis was that suburban residents of metropolitan areas with large numbers of governments would exhibit more conservative political attitudes and behaviors than their urban counterparts. According to Tiebout's hypothesis, a larger number of governments enables residents to obtain a more precise match of their preferences for particular tax and service packages.[13] Once the range of local government choices enables residents to avoid paying taxes for services and programs designed primarily to assist urban dwellers, the central city becomes less attractive. The option of choosing among numerous local governments offering varied tax and service packages encourages suburban residents to believe that by residing in "safe" communities—rather than by supporting federal programs to assist urban areas—they can escape both the problems of the city and the costs of solving those problems.

Poverty Rates

To create a score for each metropolitan area that would compare city and suburban poverty rates, the percentage of the suburban population living below the poverty line was subtracted from the percentage of the city population living below the poverty line.

The hypothesis was that the political opinions and behavior of suburbanites living in metropolitan areas with a large city-suburb difference in poverty rates would differ significantly from those of their urban counterparts. This expectation is in keeping with the argument that suburban residents react against the problems they see in the central city by increasing their support for the Republican Party and decreasing their support for federal antipoverty programs. As was the case with the variables for population change, a difference in poverty rates was expected to matter because residents of a suburb with a poverty rate near that of its city are likely to have attitudes that are closer to those of the city residents.

Racial Composition
To obtain a score on racial composition for each metropolitan area, the percentage of the city population that was black was subtracted from the percentage of the suburban population that was black.

The hypothesis was that the racial composition variable would work much the same way as the poverty variable: a large difference in racial composition between the suburbs and the city was expected to increase suburbanites' feelings of disconnection from the city and its problems. Research has shown that whites tend to view areas with large black populations as undesirable, regardless of the areas' other characteristics.[14]

Correlation between Characteristics of Metropolitan Areas

The metropolitan area characteristics described in the preceding sections are expected to be quite highly correlated with each other. In particular, Bradbury, Downs, and Small have shown that all these variables are related to suburbanization and are therefore quite strongly related to one another. Population loss in the city is associated with increased suburbanization and increased city-suburb differences in poverty rates; similarly, the percentage of the population that is black and the number of governments within the metropolitan area have all been shown to be good predictors of increased population loss in the city.[15] In addition, the age of the metropolitan area has been shown to be related to central-city decline and to the increasing suburbanization of the white middle-class population.

Are residents of suburbs in metropolitan areas with large race or poverty differentials also likely to be living in older suburbs, or

also likely to be living in suburbs with large numbers of governments? As table 32 reveals, these variables are indeed quite strongly
correlated with one another. The age of a metropolitan area is highly
and positively correlated with city-suburb differences in the percentages of poor people and in the percentages of African Americans—and, to a lesser degree, also to the number of governments. In
addition, city-suburb differences in the percentage of the population
that is poor are highly and positively correlated with large city-suburb differences in the percentage of the population that is black.
While an increase in the suburban population of a metropolitan area
is not strongly related to other variables of interest, an increase in
the city population is negatively correlated with the age and number
of governments of the metropolitan area, as well as with the city-
suburb difference in the percentage of the population that is black
and the percentage of the population that is poor. (Table 33 provides
a breakdown of the metropolitan areas according to the various characteristics discussed in this section.)

Methodology

After measures of each of the variables for all metropolitan and
suburban areas included in the NES sample had been developed, an
interaction term to reflect the relationship between each of them and
the dichotomous living-in-a-suburb variable was created. These new
variables were then used in the same models employed to examine
vote choice and opinion in chapter 5. In addition to the interaction
variables describing the metropolitan context, controls were included
for the metropolitan context alone: this step ensured that the comparisons being made were between suburban and city residents within
similar metropolitan contexts.[16] This approach is in contrast to that
used in previous sections, in which residents of particular kinds of
suburbs were being compared to all city residents, not just to those
within similar contexts.

Because of the number of variables involved and their strong
relationship to one another, no more than one suburban characteristic
was included in each model. The only exception was the growth-de-
cline variables: in order to examine whether living near a city in
decline causes city-suburban differences in political opinion (controlling for whether the suburban area is also declining), variables repre-

senting both city and suburban population change were included in the same model.

Because the variables were investigated separately, it was not possible to examine how a particular context affected attitudes while other contextual characteristics were held constant. Since these variables are all quite highly correlated with each other, including them in the same equation would have caused multi-colinearity problems—and therefore also failed to yield meaningful distinctions between contexts. Yet another approach, of questionable usefulness, would have been to create an index. Ultimately, the best option is to observe the relationship between particular contexts and political attitudes while keeping in mind that an area with any particular feature is likely to have a number of other highly related features.

Suburban Politics: Variation among Metropolitan Areas

The results of this analysis reveal that the characteristics of the metropolitan area are important for understanding city-suburban differences in vote choice, party identification, and support for government spending. City and suburban residents do not respond in like ways to similar metropolitan environments. Almost all the metropolitan contexts were related to suburban political behavior and attitudes in the expected direction.

As tables 34, 35, and 36 illustrate, living in a suburban area where the percentage of poor or black residents is lower than in the central city is consistently associated with increased support for Republican candidates for president and Congress, increased support for the Republican Party, and decreased support for spending on federal programs. As the difference in the percentage of the population that is poor or black increases, the difference in opinion between city and suburban residents also increases.

Holding all variables constant except context and observing how changes in context affect the expected values can help clarify the size of the relationship between location and political attitudes. Tables 37 and 38 show the results of this analysis for changing poverty rates and a number of different dependent variables. As the size of the gap in poverty rates between the city and the surrounding suburbs increases from 6 to 18 percent, the gap in the probability of voting for Republican candidates or supporting decreased spending on social services also increases.

The only dependent variable for which living in a metropolitan area with a large divergence in poverty rates was not also associated with city-suburb differences of opinion was Social Security spending, which has repeatedly shown itself to be unaffected by the location of respondents. Interestingly, however, a large difference in racial composition between the city and suburban area *was* associated with city-suburban differences in support for Social Security spending. Why the relationship should be different for racial composition than for poverty levels is unclear. Perhaps this finding confirms the results of studies of contemporary racial segregation: namely, that the percentage of the population that is black continues to matter in ways that other residential characteristics do not.

Suburban and city residents of older metropolitan areas also differ significantly in their support for Republican candidates, identification with the Republican Party, and support for federal spending. The older the metropolitan area, the greater the divide between city and suburban respondents. (The only exception to this pattern was, once again, Social Security spending.) The same relationship exists between the number of governments in the metropolitan area and political attitudes and behaviors: the more governments there are (taking population into account), the greater the division between the attitudes of suburban and city respondents. The two exceptions in this case are spending on food stamps and, again, on Social Security.

The variables reflecting population change are significantly related to distinct suburban opinion only in the case of presidential and congressional vote choice and party identification. In these three instances, decreases in the city population from 1980 to 1990 are associated with increasing city-suburb divergence in attitudes. In the case of congressional vote choice and party identification, the relationship between city population decline and politics is mediated somewhat by population change in the suburban areas: if the suburbs have also lost population, the city-suburban divergence in opinion begins to decline.

Although it is not possible on the basis of these models to determine which contextual characteristic is the most strongly related to city-suburb variations in attitude, it is possible to speculate. The first point to keep in mind is that the age and number of governments were expected to have an indirect rather than direct relationship to context. In other words, age and number of governments were ex-

pected to be *associated* with particular contextual characteristics—not to *be* contextual characteristics. Consequently, it makes
sense to accord them less importance than the contextual characteristics with which they are associated: percentage black, percentage
poor, and population loss. Of these three, percentage African American and percentage poor are the two variables most consistently and
significantly associated with vote choice and support for spending on
federal programs. Given their high degree of correlation, distinguishing between these two may be both impossible and pointless. However, it is worth recalling from the analysis in the first section of this
chapter that when the percentage poor and percentage black of the
suburban ring (rather than the divergence between the city and suburban ring) are included in the same equation, it is consistently
race—and not poverty—that is significantly associated with vote
choice and support for federal spending.

These results show that the divergence between city and suburban
residents in vote choice and political attitudes depends in part on the
characteristics of the metropolitan context within which the city and
surrounding suburbs are located. Models that included one metropolitan variable at a time revealed that all the location variables had
the expected relationship with the dependent variables. The attitudes
of suburban and city residents diverged more sharply in older metropolitan areas, in metropolitan areas that had more governments, in
areas where cities were losing population, and in areas where there
were large city-suburb differences in the percentage of the population
that was poor and the percentage that was black.

Clearly, city and suburban residents are not responding to a
shared metropolitan environment in the same way. Suburban residents do not appear to view their fortunes as being tied to those of
nearby city dwellers, and they do not respond to the plight of the city
with increased support for programs that might benefit urban residents. In fact, the opposite is true: the more the fortunes of the city
and surrounding suburbs diverge, the more likely suburban residents
are to favor Republican candidates for office and to oppose spending
on federal programs.

This finding supports the argument that the distinctive political
attitudes of suburbanites are, in part, a reaction against the conditions
that exist in the nearby city. The finding may also help to explain why,
as discussed in chapter 2, a distinctive suburban politics developed
later rather than sooner. It was during the 1980s that the gap between

suburbs and cities grew on a number of socioeconomic measures, and it was during the late 1980s and early 1990s that a corresponding divergence in political behavior and attitudes—which persists even after individual-level characteristics are taken into account—emerged.

- Suburban residents are more supportive of the Republican Party and Republican candidates and less supportive of government spending than city residents, all else held constant.
- In suburbs with more citylike features, the political views of residents differ less from those of urban dwellers than do those of residents of more traditional suburban areas.
- An increase in the percentage of the suburban population that is black is associated with a decrease in the city-suburb gap in
    The probability of voting for or identifying as a Republican.
    Support for spending on programs to assist blacks.
    Scores on the feeling thermometer measuring attitudes toward welfare recipients.
- If the suburban area has experienced population loss, there are two different outcomes:
    A decrease in the city-suburb gap in the probability of voting for or identifying as a Republican.
    An increase in the city-suburb gap in support for spending on programs to assist blacks and in scores on the feeling thermometer measuring attitudes toward welfare recipients.
- The greater the divergence between a city and its suburban ring in terms of population loss, the percentage of the population that is African American, and the percentage that is poor,
    The greater the divergence in the probability of voting for or identifying as a Republican.
    The greater the divergence in the probability of supporting spending on federal programs, other than Social Security.

Figure 6-1. Summary of Findings in Chapter 6

The Causal Connection

As was discussed in some depth in chapter 4, findings that confirm a relationship between living in a suburb and distinctive political attitudes and vote choice do not necessarily answer questions about the direction of causality of this relationship. Are those who choose to live in the suburbs different initially from those who choose to stay in the cities? In other words, is suburbanization simply the geographic sorting of already dissimilar individuals? Or is there something about the experience of living in a suburb that changes people who are initially indistinguishable from their urban counterparts?

Although the findings presented here are interesting regardless of the direction of causality, the fact that the political attitudes of suburban and urban residents diverge more in some metropolitan contexts than in others suggests that suburbanites are indeed being affected by the environment in which they live.

Deciding to live in the suburbs rather than the city within a particular metropolitan area may be correlated with distinctive political behavior, but it seems much less likely that the decision to live in any particular metropolitan area is correlated with political behavior. In other words, while the decision to live in the city of Miami or in the surrounding suburbs may be related to political orientation, the initial decision to live in the Miami metropolitan area is much more likely to be related to things like job opportunities or family ties. Given this supposition, the finding that city and suburban residents differ more in some kinds of metropolitan areas than in others suggests that something happens after, rather than before, they move.

The findings for metropolitan areas that are older or that have lots of governments are particularly supportive of this view. The fact that I live in a metropolitan area that has lots of governments probably has little to do with my political beliefs. But the fact that when I live in the suburbs of this type of metropolitan area I am more different from my urban counterparts than I would be if I lived in a metropolitan area with fewer governments suggests that something about living in this particular suburb has affected my politics.

While this argument is persuasive, an alternative hypothesis cannot be ruled out. The more local governments there are within a metropolitan area, the more alternatives there are to the central city and the greater the likelihood that I will prefer one of these alternatives. It may be, then, that the geographic sorting of already different individuals is simply performed more effectively in metropolitan areas with lots of local governments, and that this accounts for the greater divergence.

Understanding the diversity of suburban areas and the diversity of metropolitan contexts can help explain the ways in which the political attitudes of city and suburban residents differ. It can also shed light on the consequences, for national politics, of a distinctive suburban politics. The next two chapters deal with this issue in more detail. Chapter 7 looks at congressional politics in an age when increasing numbers of members of Congress represent predominantly suburban districts. Chapter 8 provides a closer look at the relationship between suburban voting behavior and party politics.

Notes

1. For a discussion of this research, see chapter 2.

2. See, for example, Mark Baldassare, *Trouble in Paradise: The Suburban Transformation in America* (New York: Columbia University Press, 1986); Barry Schwartz, *The Changing Face of the Suburbs* (Chicago: University of Chicago Press, 1976); Louis H. Masotti and Jeffrey K. Hadden, eds., *The Urbanization of the Suburbs* (Beverly Hills, Calif.: Sage Publications, 1973).

3. See, for example, Thomas Byrne Edsall and Mary D. Edsall, *Chain Reaction: The Impact of Race, Rights, and Taxes on American Politics* (New York: W.W. Norton, 1992); Robert B. Reich, *Tales of a New America* (New York: Times Books, 1987); William Schneider, "The Suburban Century Begins: The Real Meaning of the 1992 Election," *Atlantic Monthly,* July 1992.

4. Joseph Zikmund II, "A Comparison of Political Attitude and Activity Patterns in Central Cities and Suburbs," *Public Opinion Quarterly* 31, no. 1 (spring 1967).

5. Douglas S. Massey and Nancy A. Denton, *American Apartheid: Segregation and the Making of the Underclass* (Cambridge, Mass.: Harvard University Press, 1993).

6. Katherine L. Bradbury, Anthony Downs, and Kenneth A. Small, *Urban Decline and the Future of American Cities* (Washington, D.C.: Brookings Institution Press, 1982).

7. The equation used in the model was as follows: Y = constant + Xß [individual-level variables] + a$_2$suburb + a$_3$(suburb * percent black) + a$_4$(suburb * percent poor) + a$_5$(suburb * declining)

8. In this chapter, party identification is not included as a control variable but is treated exclusively as a dependent variable. As was the case in the previous chapter, the inclusion of party identification as an independent variable weakens the relationship between suburbanization and political attitudes and behavior, but only occasionally is the effect sufficient to prevent living in a suburb from being statistically significant. Since it is a premise of this book that for at least part of the relationship the causal arrow extends from attitudes to party identification, and since the effect of treating party identification as a control variable has been discussed previously, results are reported in this chapter for models that do not include party identification as a control.

9. Ed Reilly, quoted in Edsall and Edsall, *Chain Reaction*, 226.

10. Donald J. Bogue, *Population Growth in Standard Metropolitan Areas 1900–1950* (Washington, D.C.: GPO, 1953); Robert M. Stein, *Urban Alternatives: Public and Private Markets in the Provision of Local Services* (Pittsburgh: University of Pittsburgh Press, 1990).

11. Bradbury, Downs, and Small, *Urban Decline*.

12. These measures for the years from 1980 to 1990 may be somewhat unrepresentative since a number of cities that had been experiencing severe decline before 1980 began to gain population in the decade that followed. (These cities are Boston, Des Moines, Fort Wayne, Grand Rapids, New Haven–West Haven, New York, San Francisco–Oakland, Seattle–Everett, and Worcester.) Given that several decades of severe decline are not likely to have been counteracted by a period of modest population increase, the growth measures for this period may not accurately represent the state of the metropolitan area. However, since the rates of growth in these cities were still relatively small, it was hoped that they would remain substantially differentiated from growth rates in areas with high and consistent growth.

13. Charles Tiebout, "A Pure Theory of Local Expenditures," *Journal of Political Economy* 64, no. 5 (October 1956). Bradbury, Downs, and Small found evidence that when more local governments exist in a metropolitan area ("the more local was local government"), suburbanization increases (*Urban Decline*, p. 102). This finding supports the idea that the presence of more governments makes the central city relatively less attractive as a place to live.

14. Massey and Denton, *American Apartheid*, 88–96.

15. Bradbury, Downs, and Small, *Urban Decline*.

16. The equation used was as follows: Y = constant + Xß (individual-level variables) + a$_2$metro context + a$_3$(metro context * suburb).

CHAPTER SEVEN

Suburban Representation in Congress

The parking lots of the two big supermarkets in this Houston suburb are crowded with mini-vans and four-wheel-drive wagons like Jeep Cherokees and Ford Explorers. The average selling price of a house is $100,000. People brag about the high achievement scores in the local schools and the low crime rate. . . . In November, for the first time in recent memory, they elected a Republican. . . . And they rejected . . . the Democrat who had represented them in Congress since 1952.

> *New York Times*, "A Houston Suburb That Said No to a
> Democrat, after Forty-Two Years"

Probably no one is more surprised at David A. Roberti's election campaign through the suburban tracts of the San Fernando Valley than the veteran Democratic State Senator himself. Long a leading liberal in the California political firmament, Senator Roberti now boasts of his backing of three new bills in the Legislature to toughen penalties for looting and arson, and he eagerly poses with police officers. . . . Senator Roberti's passage from urban liberal to suburban law-and-order candidate echoes the trend of urban politics today . . . in both Congress and state legislatures.

> Robert Reinhold,
> "Chasing Votes from Big Cities to the Suburbs"

Chapter 4 discussed the difficulty of sorting out the causal direction of the relationship between living in a suburb and distinctive political behavior and attitudes. That chapter also noted, however, that regardless of the direction of causality, the geographic organization of political representation in America gives this distinctive politics important implications. Because members of Congress are elected to represent constituencies that are geographically defined, when people with distinctive political views are clustered together geographically, their views are more likely to find expression at the national level than if the same people were distributed evenly throughout the land. This assumes, of course, that the politicians who represent the residents of these geographic areas will put their constituents' interests forward in national politics.

Attributing significance to the geographic as well as partisan affiliations of politicians is not a new idea. Before the 1960s, in discussions of both the national and state legislatures, the possibility that rural interests had excessive influence was a matter of great concern. When the topic of suburbanization first began to interest political scientists, some suggested that the shift in Congress from urban to suburban representation could be as significant as the shift from rural to urban power had been.[1]

However, like much of the research on the political behavior of suburbanites, the research into suburban representation in Congress has produced inconclusive and sometimes contradictory results. In 1969, on the basis of a collection of case studies of congressional behavior, Cleaveland concluded that while party was the most important factor in determining the members' behavior, constituency type played an important role in explaining variations in party loyalty.[2] In 1974, *Congressional Quarterly* classified congressional districts as urban, suburban, or rural and examined Americans for Democratic Action scores and votes on certain issues for divisions along constituency rather than party lines. While suburban Democrats generally voted more like urban Democrats than like suburban Republicans—and suburban Republicans voted more like urban Republicans—"suburban members seemed to be taking a position of their own" on some issues. For example, on mass-transit operating subsidies, urban renewal, and farm subsidies, support differed among Democrats and Republicans depending on which type of district they represented.[3]

Caraley has undertaken a more recent effort to look systematically at the relationship between population movement out of cities and changes in congressional behavior.[4] In keeping with earlier research, however, Caraley found that while differences in the composition of the constituency (that is, largely urban versus largely suburban) have some effect on the behavior of members of Congress, the impact is small in comparison to that of party differences. In a study of patterns of congressional support for urban aid proposals during the Carter administration and in another study of congressional support for Reagan's New Federalism, Caraley argues that what matters most with respect to support for urban programs is the number of Democrats in Congress. Region—and then the composition of the districts—are a distant second and third.[5] Caraley speculates, however, that this pattern may change over time, as fiscal constraints make Democrats from suburban districts less willing to follow the party tradition of support for cities, and as the increasing suburbanization of the electorate diminishes the level of presidential leadership and initiative in the increasingly vote-poor area of urban aid.[6]

While comparisons of the voting behavior of members in each category of district have not, to date, revealed overwhelming evidence of a distinctive suburban behavior, some other observers of congressional behavior have suggested that the increasingly suburban nature of districts is indeed important. Danielson explains the federal government's failure to support the opening of the suburbs to poor people as in part a consequence of increasing suburban influence at the national level:

> Candidates who succeed in these increasingly suburban constituencies tend to be recruited from suburbia where their political perspectives have been shaped by the localistic and exclusionary preoccupations of their constituents. The result, as one influential suburban politician has written, is a steady shift in "the balance of political power and influence . . . to those political leaders who articulate and strive to maintain the suburban way of life."[7]

Similarly, Dreier, describing obstacles to the establishment of a progressive urban policy, points to the decline in urban representation in Congress and the corresponding increase in suburban representation: "Members of Congress who represent suburban areas may have some personal sympathy, but less political motivation, to vote to spend their constituents' tax dollars to alleviate urban problems."[8]

In his most recent discussion of Washington's treatment of the cities, Caraley discusses the prospects for increased aid in the future and concludes that "finally and perhaps most fundamentally, it depends on elite beliefs and broad public opinion—essentially the dominant public philosophy—about the responsibility of the federal government for dealing with problems of individual and family poverty and distress and for alleviating extreme disparities among local and state governments."[9] The results presented in chapters 5 and 6 suggest that as the population becomes increasingly suburbanized, the dominant public philosophy becomes increasingly hostile to the idea of a large federal role in the alleviation of problems that are located, for the most part, in cities. In addition, the finding that people who live in the suburbs are more likely, all else held constant, to vote for Republican members of Congress suggests that even the most powerful predictor of congressional support for or opposition to programs that benefit cities—party—is in part a consequence of how suburban the district is.

Change over Time

The first step in assessing the impact of suburbanization on congressional representation is to see how the composition of districts has actually changed over time.[10] Two questions are important: First, has the number of predominantly suburban districts increased relative to that of predominantly urban or rural districts? Second, has the number of "mixed districts"—that is, districts where representatives are required to represent the interests of two or more types of constituencies—declined?

This chapter relies on the same definition of *suburban* that was developed for the analysis of public opinion: suburban dwellers are those who reside within the metropolitan area but outside the boundary of the central city. Classifying congressional districts as predominantly urban or suburban, however, means selecting a threshold percentage of the population that must be of one type or the other in order for the district to qualify as predominantly urban or suburban. In this chapter, the multivariate analysis is based on the actual percentage of the population that is suburban, which avoids the issue of thresholds. However, the summary statistics are based on two thresholds, both of which have been used in previous studies of congressional districts and thus allow for useful comparisons over time. The first of these classifies congressional districts as predominantly suburban when 60 percent or more of the population lives in the suburbs, as predominantly urban when 60 percent or more lives within the central city, as predominantly rural when 60 percent or more lives outside the metropolitan area, and as "mixed" when none of these criteria are met. The second classification scheme uses 50 percent as the threshold, which has the advantage of leaving fewer districts in the mixed category but raises other questions—principally, to what extent can a district that is only 51 percent suburban really be called suburban?[11]

Over time, as shown in table 39, the number of suburban districts has increased and the number of districts in the other categories has decreased, regardless of the classification scheme. In 1973, congressional districts were still fairly evenly divided among the three types, with 102 (23 percent) classified as urban, 131 (30 percent) as suburban, and 130 (30 percent) as rural. However, by 1993 the suburban category was about two and one-half times the size of either the rural or the urban category.

Although both classification schemes reveal growth in the number of suburban districts, the mixed category is much smaller under the 50 percent benchmark than under the 60 percent benchmark. As a comparison of the suburban figure under the two classification schemes shows, in one-third of those districts classified as mixed in 1973 under the 60 percent scheme, the majority of the population was actually suburban.

It is now possible to answer the two questions posed earlier about changes in the composition of congressional districts. Clearly, the number of predominantly suburban districts has increased over time—which means that more and more members of Congress are elected from districts where more than 50 percent of the population is suburban.

With respect to the second question, both classification schemes show an overall decline in the number of mixed districts. Although this decline has not been huge (under the 50 percent scheme, the number of mixed districts actually increased between 1973 and 1985), a look at the "change" figures in table 39 suggests that after 1985, the decline increased in significance. Between 1973 and 1985, the increase in the number of suburban districts occurred mainly at the expense of rural districts: although the number of urban and mixed districts declined, the drop was slight in comparison with the drop in the number of rural districts. But between 1985 and 1993, the continuing suburban increase owed much less to a decline in the number of rural districts and much more to a decline in the number of mixed districts, as well as to continuing decline in the number of urban districts. This pattern suggests that increasing suburban representation might have had a different impact on policy between 1973 and 1985 than between 1985 and 1993. During the first period, rural districts were primarily replaced by suburban ones, but during the second period, decreases in urban and mixed representation fed the growth in suburban representation.

Consequences of Increased Suburban Representation

The findings just discussed show that the number of predominantly suburban districts has been on the increase since the 1960s and 1970s—the years when much of the research on suburban representation in Congress was done. Consequently, the impact of recent changes in the number of suburban congressional districts has been largely unexplored. In a recent article exploring changes in central-city representation, Wolman and Marckini similarly found that the biggest change in representation in Congress had been the large increase in suburban constituencies.[12] In addition, they suggested that the power of central cities had been diluted by a decrease not only in numbers but in the voting cohesion among members who represent urban districts. While these findings suggest that changing geographic representation has policy consequences, they leave unanswered a number of questions about the precise impact of increasing suburban representation. A 1974 *Congressional Quarterly* article exploring the behavior of members from suburban districts was entitled "Suburbs: Potential but Unrealized House Influence." The question is whether, twenty years and many more suburban districts later, this potential was realized.

This section of the chapter explores some of the questions raised by previous research and by contemporary claims about the influence of suburbanization on congressional behavior. Do members of Congress who represent suburban districts behave differently from those who represent urban districts? Or are any perceived differences attributable to party affiliation rather than to constituency? Finally, even if party affiliation plays a large role in explaining the distinctive behavior of suburban members of Congress, is party affiliation in some sense attributable to increasing suburbanization?

Methodology

To answer these questions satisfactorily and to distinguish between the effects of party and those of suburbanization, it was necessary to use multivariate analysis rather than to simply examine cross-tabulations of district characteristics and congressional behavior. Consequently, the data set combines variables that describe important features of congressional districts with information about the political party and voting behavior of the member from that district.[13]

Four dependent variables were used in the analysis: whether the district was represented by a Republican or a Democrat; the proportion of the district that voted Democratic; Poole-Rosenthal Scores, a measure of ideology; and the degree of support for positions advocated by the National League of Cities (NLC).[14] As with the analyses in chapter 4, party was treated as both an independent and a dependent variable, under the premise that suburbanization affects the voting behavior of members of Congress both indirectly—through increasing the likelihood that the member is from a particular party—and directly.

Using support for NLC positions as a measure of support for urban interests raises some problems because the NLC represents not only large cities but also much smaller (that is, suburban) cities. However, the organization is associated closely enough with urban interests for the selection of bills that it supports to serve as an interesting dependent variable. In addition, because NLC positions do not necessarily represent traditionally "liberal" or "conservative" interests, this variable provides a useful contrast to ideology scores. For example, the NLC's arguments against unfunded mandates imposed on local governments sometimes place it in opposition to traditional liberal interests.

The independent variables used in this analysis are those that are commonly thought to explain the behavior of members of Congress:[15]

- Election characteristics: the Democratic proportion of the major-party vote; whether an incumbent holds the seat or it is an open seat
- Member characteristics: party and length of service
- District characteristics: percentage of the electorate that is over age sixty-five; percentage of the electorate that is African American; median family income of the electorate; percentage with at least a high school education; percentage living in the suburbs, cities, or countryside; and whether the district is in a southern state.

To mirror the time period used for the voting behavior analysis, district data for the 101st through the 103rd Congresses were pooled.

Most of the district characteristics included in the multivariate analysis were also expected to be characteristics of suburban areas. Given what is known about suburbia, those districts that are more suburban can be expected to have fewer African American residents, higher median incomes, and more highly educated residents. The correlations reported in table 40 illustrate that these expectations are valid.

These variables were included, on the one hand, as control variables: to see whether the percentage of the district population that is suburban matters beyond the fact that it increases the likelihood that the district will have fewer African Americans, a higher median income, and more constituents with at least a high school diploma. On the other hand, the fact that these variables in part *describe* the suburban environment means that their relationship with the dependent variables of interest should also be taken into account in any consideration of suburbanization and congressional behavior. Thus, in the earlier analysis, the race, income, and education variables represented individual-level characteristics, and their relationship to political attitudes was contrasted with the relationship between a contextual variable (how suburban is the respondent's location?) and political attitudes. In this chapter, the race, income, education, and suburban variables play a different role: all are contextual in the sense that they describe a congressional district rather than an individual.

The Impact of Suburban Constituents on Congressional Behavior

The results of the analysis support the idea that congressional districts with large suburban populations are more likely to elect Republicans and that their Republican representatives have more conservative voting records. The next three sections take a more detailed look at these findings.

Party

Predominantly suburban congressional districts are clearly more likely than predominantly urban districts to be represented by Republicans. Although representatives from districts that are more than 50 percent suburban are about evenly divided between the Democratic and Republican Parties, among districts that are more than 50 percent urban the representatives are much more likely to be from the Democratic Party (table 41).

But does this pattern persist when other characteristics of suburban areas are held constant? As table 42 reveals, even after other characteristics that might be expected to determine whether a district will be represented by a Republican or Democrat are controlled for, the "suburban-ness" of the district remains an important predictor. This finding is not unexpected, given the increased propensity of suburban residents to vote Republican, all else held constant, that was demonstrated in chapters 5 and 6.

To clarify the meaning, in real terms, of this statistically significant coefficient for suburban-ness, it is useful to hold the other variables constant and compare a less suburban to a more suburban district. As table 43 illustrates, if the other variables are held constant at their mean and the percentage of the population residing in the suburbs increases, so does the probability that a district will be represented by a Republican member of Congress. For example, a non-Southern district with an open seat, mean education and income, and a 5 percent African American population has a 17 percent probability of electing a Republican to Congress if only 10 percent of the population is suburban and the other 90 percent is urban. If the percentages are reversed while the other variables are held constant, the district has a 31 percent probability of electing a Republican to Congress.

Furthermore, the association between the degree of suburbanization and the election of a Republican congressional representative persists even when the party of the incumbent member of Congress is controlled for. Given that the incumbent's party is in part a consequence of how suburban the district is, the actual relationship between the percentage of the district's population that is suburban and the expected party of the representative is probably even larger.

Similarly, not only the final choice of candidate but also the proportion of the vote that the Democratic candidate wins seems to be partly a function of the district's level of suburbanization. The mean proportion of votes that go to the Democratic Party is over 20 percentage points lower in districts where a majority of constituents are suburban than in districts where a majority are urban: 49.6 in the suburban districts versus 70.2 in the urban districts. This difference continues to exist, although at a diminished level, even when other variables are controlled for (table 44).

As the percentage of the district's population that lives in the suburbs increases, the expected Democratic share of the vote for Congress declines. For every percentage point increase in the level of suburbanization, the Democratic share of the vote declines by just under one-tenth of a percentage point. This means, for example, that a district that is 50 percent suburban would, all else held constant, have an expected Democratic vote about four and one-half percentage points lower than a district with no suburban population. Similarly, a district that is 100 percent suburban would have an expected Democratic vote nine percentage points lower than a district with no suburban population. While this is not a huge difference, it is clearly enough to tip the balance in favor of one candidate or another, and it is comparable in size to the effect of such independent variables as whether the district is in the South. In addition, the actual relationship is probably stronger than reported here. Since it has been demonstrated that the probability of electing a Republican representative is affected by suburbanization, the variable that matters the most for explaining the Democratic share of the vote—whether there is a Republican incumbent—cannot be considered completely unrelated to the level of suburbanization.

Districts that are predominantly suburban, all else held constant, are generally less likely to vote for Democratic congressional candidates and more likely to send a Republican to represent them in Congress. However, the question remains whether the Democrats who represent such districts act more like Republicans or like Democrats from urban districts. Conversely, do Republicans representing urban areas behave more like Democrats? The next section addresses these questions.

Ideology

When Poole-Rosenthal scores for representatives from predominantly suburban districts are compared with those for representatives from predominantly urban districts, the greater conservatism of suburban representatives is clear. The mean score for House members from suburban areas is .009, while the mean score for members from urban areas is −.266.[16] However, since representatives from predominantly suburban areas are much more likely to be Republican, a large amount of this difference is related to party. When the mean scores are compared within party lines, the difference between suburban and urban representatives is greatly diminished.

As table 45 shows, although there are some difference between types of districts, these differences are much smaller than those that distinguish representatives from different political parties. For example, the difference in mean Poole-Rosenthal scores between Democrats who represent districts that are over 50 percent suburban and Democrats who represent districts that are over 50 percent urban is only .085 points, whereas the difference between Democrats and Republicans who both represent primarily suburban districts is .628 points. Table 45 also includes scores for districts that are even more heavily suburban or urban (more than 70 percent), but the results are substantially the same: some small differences exist within the parties, depending on district type, but they are overwhelmed by the large differences between the parties. Interestingly, district type seems to make more difference in the Democrats' Poole-Rosenthal scores than in those of Republicans, but again the numbers involved are small.

Given the relatively small differences found in mean Poole-Rosenthal scores once party is taken into account, it seemed likely that the multivariate analysis would not reveal a strong relationship between the percentage of the district's population that is suburban and the expected Poole-Rosenthal score of the representative. Table 46 bears out this expectation. While the suburban coefficient was statistically significant at the 0.05 level, the coefficient was small enough that the predicted effect was also fairly small: a member from a 100 percent suburban district would be expected to have a Poole-Rosenthal score only .04 points higher than that of a member from a 100 percent urban district, all else held constant.

At the same time, however, as noted earlier, the party of the representative and the percentage of the vote that was Democratic both result in part from the district's degree of suburbanization. If this indirect effect of suburbanization is taken into account, the relationship between the size of the suburban constituency and member ideology would obviously be stronger. Another important point to keep in mind is that the district's percentage of constituents who are African American, percentage of constituents who are over sixty-five years old, and percentage of constituents with at least a high school education all have a strong and significant relationship to the Poole-Rosenthal scores for members of Congress. Given the correlation between these variables and the degree of suburbanization, it is hard to argue that the level of suburbanization has only a slight relationship to ideology in Congress. However, once these environmental characteristics—which help, in part, to distinguish urban and suburban environments—are taken into account, the degree of suburbanization still retains some explanatory power.

Support for Programs for the Poor and for Cities

With the increase in suburban representation has come an increasing willingness in Congress to cut programs aimed at cities or at the poor more generally. The 1980s marked significant declines in the amount of federal aid to cities. As a result of budget cuts enacted during Ronald Reagan's years in the White House, federal aid as a percentage of state-local budgets, which between 1958 and 1978 had risen from 11 to 26 percent, had fallen, by 1988, to 17 percent.[17] While some researchers have pointed out that the 1980s budget cuts never actually reached the levels that Reagan set out to achieve, the cuts that were put into effect disproportionately affected programs aimed at cities.

One study of state and local government responses to cuts in federal aid found that "the more highly targeted a program was on the poor, the more likely it was to be cut by the national government."[18] Similarly, Caraley identified federal government programs that were designed to alleviate problems associated primarily with cities—poverty and unemployment, physical decay, deteriorating economic bases, education, transportation, and the need for general financial assistance—and found that between 1980 and 1990, spending in constant dollars on these programs declined by 46 percent, or around $26 billion.[19]

Programs of importance to cities—such as general revenue sharing, urban development action grants, and the Comprehensive Employment and Training Act—were all eliminated completely during the Reagan years. Even the more positive assessments of the experience of cities during the Reagan years do not ultimately contradict the general picture of a federal government that was less and less responsive to cities and to the needs of those who lived in them.[20]

While these cuts in the programs that benefited cities and poor people occurred during the period of increased suburban and decreased urban representation in Congress, can it be said conclusively that the one is a consequence of the other? As with the Poole-Rosenthal scores, a breakdown of support for these cuts among suburban and urban representatives shows a clear relationship between degree of suburbanization and voting record—but, as was *not* the case with the Poole-Rosenthal scores, the introduction of other factors (in particular, political party) dissolves the relationship. For example, Caraley's work examining congressional support for the bills that composed Reagan's New Federalism found large differences between suburban and urban members of Congress.[21] However, these differences were negligible once political party was taken into account.

Similar patterns were revealed by the analysis of congressional support scores for programs identified by the National League of Cities as important votes in the 101st through 103rd Congresses.[22] Representatives from the suburbs were less supportive of these bills than were members from the cities. The mean NLC score for representatives of predominantly suburban districts was 53, while the mean score for members from predominantly urban districts was 68. However, once political party and the other variables used in the analysis of Poole-Rosenthal scores were included in a multivariate analysis, any independent relationship between the percentage of constituents that lived in the suburbs and a member's support score disappeared (table 47).

Once again, however, it should be noted that despite the failure of the degree-of-suburbanization variable to achieve statistical significance, variables that are, in part, a consequence of the district's degree of suburbanization—the party of the representative and the proportion of the vote that goes to the Democratic Party—play a significant role in predicting support for NLC positions. When these political variables are omitted from the model, the percentage of the district that is suburban is significantly related to the representative's expected score on the NLC index.

Conclusion

This chapter has shown that congressional representatives from predominantly suburban districts are more likely to be Republicans and are less liberal and less supportive of the NLC agenda than representatives from predominantly urban districts. These patterns persist even when other characteristics of the congressional district—median income, percentage of residents with a high school education or above, percentage of residents who are African American—are taken into account. Furthermore, these other characteristics are also related to suburbanization. To a large extent, suburbanization involves geographic sorting along lines of race and income. It is the geographic clusters of African Americans and high-income people that in part explain the voting behavior of members of Congress. However, in the case of votes favored by the NLC, the distinctions between suburban and urban representatives disappear once the party of the representative and the percentage of the district vote that was Democratic are taken into account.

Clearly, the strongest predictor of a member of Congress's voting behavior is political party, but the political party of the representative is in part a consequence of how suburban the district is. Similarly, the Democratic proportion of the vote is also a strong predictor of a member's voting behavior and also appears to be in part a consequence of the level of suburbanization in the district: the more suburban the district, the lower the vote share for the Democratic candidate, if all else is held constant.

The strongest implication of increasing suburban representation thus appears to be the advantage given to the Republican Party. In many ways, this view corresponds to what researchers in the 1960s and 1970s expected to find and did not—that increasing suburbanization leads to Republican dominance. However, a Republican advantage should not necessarily be interpreted as a prediction of Republican dominance: in a two-party system, the Democratic Party will move toward the Republicans if that seems necessary in order to win elections. To really understand the meaning of increasing suburbanization and the advantage it seems to give the Republicans, it is essential to consider what it is about the Republican Party's message that attracts suburban voters and what evidence there is that the Democratic Party is moving to adopt these "suburban" positions. These issues will be covered in the next chapter.

Notes

1. Richard Lehne, "Shape of the Future," *National Civic Review* 58, (September 1969):351–55; Thomas P. Murphy, *The New Politics of Congress* (Lexington, Mass.: Lexington Books, 1974).

2. Frederic N. Cleaveland, *Congress and Urban Problems: A Casebook of the Legislative Process* (Washington, D.C.: Brookings Institution Press, 1969).

3. "Suburbs: Potential but Unrealized House Influence," *Congressional Quarterly Weekly Report*, 6 April 1974, 878–80. This analysis considered only the percentages of votes cross-tabulated by party and the percentage of constituents living in the suburbs; it did not try to control for other features of congressional districts. A more recent example of district type prevailing over party loyalty is support for sampling by the Census Bureau. While the Republican position was against sampling, Republican representative Chris Shays supported sampling because it would benefit urban districts like the one he represents. See Christina Duff, "Plans for Census 'Sampling' Anger GOP in Congress," *Wall Street Journal*, 12 June 1997, p. A20.

4. Demetrios Caraley, "Carter, Congress, and the Cities," in *Urban Policy Making,* ed. Dale Rogers Marshall (Beverly Hills, Calif.: Sage Publications, 1979); Demetrios Caraley and Yvette R. Schlussel, "Congress and Reagan's New Federalism," *Publius: The Journal of Federalism* 16, no. 1 (winter 1986).

5. Caraley reaches this conclusion by grouping members of Congress according to the criteria of interest (party, region, and constituency) and then comparing the percentage of members within each group who supported urban aid programs. The largest gap in support is found when support scores for Democrats are compared with those for Republicans.

6. Caraley, "Carter, Congress, and the Cities," 92–95.

7. Michael D. Danielson, *The Politics of Exclusion* (New York: Columbia University Press, 1976), 201.

8. Peter Dreier, "Putting Cities on the National Agenda," *Urban Affairs Review* 30, no. 5 (May 1995).

9. Demetrios Caraley, "Washington Abandons the Cities," *Political Science Quarterly* 107, no. 1 (spring 1992):17.

10. This section is based on data kindly provided by David C. Huckabee, of the Congressional Research Service, who combined his own data analysis with earlier analyses from *Congressional Quarterly.* See David C. Huckabee, "Congressional Districts of the 99th Congress Classified on an Urban to Rural Continuum" (report prepared for the Congressional Research Service, 9 September 1985); see also "Suburbs: Potential but Unrealized House Influence."

11. For a discussion of the merits of various ways of classifying congressional districts, see Huckabee, "Congressional Districts."

12. Harold Wolman and Lisa Marckini, "Changes in Central-City Representation and Influence in Congress Since the 1960s," *Urban Affairs Review* 34, no. 2 (November 1998).

13. For data on the majority of these variables the author is extremely grateful to David Lublin for allowing use of his comprehensive congressional district data set. The data describing the suburban character of the districts were provided by David Huckabee of the Congressional Research Service.

14. Poole and Rosenthal used roll-call votes to develop a measure of the ideology of members of Congress. Because they include all roll-call votes in their model (except those in which the minority garnered less than 2.5 percent of the vote), these scores do a better job than other ratings of congressional voting (for example, those of the Americans for Democratic Action) in measuring the ideological placement of representatives. In addition, because the measure is scaled to allow comparisons across years, it is appropriate to use it with a data set that pools data from several congressional sessions. See Keith Poole and Howard Rosenthal, "Patterns of Congressional Voting," *American Journal of Political Science* 35, no. 1 (February 1991); David Lublin, *The Paradox of Representation: Racial Gerrymandering and Minority Interests in Congress* (Princeton, N.J.: Princeton University Press, 1997), 67–68, 115.

15. See Lublin, *Paradox of Representation*.

16. The Poole-Rosenthal scores in this data set range from –.79 to .71, with a mean score of –.041 and a standard deviation around the mean of .34.

17. E. Blaine Liner, ed., *A Decade of Devolution: Perspectives on State-Local Relations* (Washington, D.C.: Urban Institute Press, 1989), 6.

18. Michael E. Bell, ed., *Research in Urban Economics: State and Local Finance in an Era of New Federalism* (Greenwich, Conn.: JAI Press, 1988), 146.

19. Caraley, "Washington Abandons the Cities."

20. Andrew R. Parker, "Patterns of Federal Urban Spending: Central Cities and Their Suburbs, 1983–1992," *Urban Affairs Review* 31, no. 2 (November 1995); George E. Peterson, "Urban Policy and the Cyclical Behavior of Cities," in *Reagan and the Cities*, ed. George E. Peterson and Carol W. Lewis (Washington, D.C.: Urban Institute Press, 1986).

21. Caraley and Schlussel, "Congress and Reagan's New Federalism."

22. Data supplied by the Center for Policy and Federal Relations, National League of Cities.

CHAPTER EIGHT

Party Politics and the Suburbs

Throughout this book, a strong and consistent relationship has emerged between political party and living in a suburb. People who live in suburbs are more likely than their urban counterparts to vote for Republican congressional and presidential candidates and to identify themselves as supporters of the Republican Party. In addition, as the percentage of the electorate that lives in the suburbs increases, congressional districts are increasingly likely to be represented by Republicans. In earlier discussion of the suburbs, the expectation that such a relationship between Republicans and suburbanization existed prompted predictions that the Republicans would come to dominate American politics. However, despite the fact that the Democrats succeeded in electing a president only once between 1968 and 1992, and despite the 1994 congressional landslide in favor of the Republicans, the GOP has not achieved undisputed dominance, even as the suburban share of the electorate has grown.

This chapter considers in greater detail the relationship between party and suburbanization. Why are suburbanites more supportive of the Republican Party and candidates? To what extent is the Republican message designed to appeal more to suburban dwellers than to comparable residents of cities? In addition, to what extent is the message of the Democratic Party shaped by the desire to appeal to suburban voters? In a two-party system, the second party—in order to avoid remaining in a losing position—can be expected to adapt to a situation in which the majority of the electorate is suburban. How has the Democratic Party attempted to mitigate the Republicans' suburban advantage?

Devolution: A Suburban Approach to Social Policy

The relationship between race, class, and competition between parties has been well documented.[1] What this chapter will demonstrate is that place entered the political dialogue in the course of this party competition. During the 1980s, the Republican Party discussed social policy in place-specific terms that were calculated to appeal more strongly to suburban than to urban voters. In the American context, the strong relationship between residence, race, and class ensures on the one hand that government policies that deal explicitly with race and class will have a "place" dimension—and on the other hand that policies that deal explicitly with location will have a race and class dimension. Given the tight interconnection between these three factors, it becomes less surprising that urban and suburban voters differ on vote choice.

Place entered the social policy debate through the argument that responsibility for social policy needed to be turned back to lower levels of government. Discussions about which level of government should perform certain functions often draw on a particular conception of what local communities are like—a conception that stresses the appeal of neighbor helping neighbor and ignores the racial, ethnic, and socioeconomic homogeneity of many communities. This chapter suggests that the competition for middle-class voters and Reagan Democrats involved not only conceptions of the race and class of these voters but also a recognition of their status as suburbanites.

Reagan and Place

After fifty years of continuous growth in federal power, Ronald Reagan became the first post–New Deal president to make the return of power to states and localities a central tenet of his agenda. This shift occurred during the 1980s—the time when the statistical analysis con-

ducted for this book found the strongest relationship between suburban living and support for the Republican presidential candidate.[2]

In his inaugural address, Reagan promised that he would "curb
the size and the influence of the federal establishment and . . . demand recognition of the distinction between the powers granted to
the federal government and those reserved to the states or to the
people."[3] He sounded a similar theme in his 1982 state of the union
address, when he proposed turning responsibility for welfare and
food stamps back to the states: "Together, after 50 years of taking
power from the hands of the people in their states and local communities, we have started returning power and resources to them."
Acknowledging that some might doubt the ability of states and localities to take over these responsibilities, Reagan claimed that there
was no cause for worry: "We . . . believe in the integrity, decency, and
sound good sense of grassroots Americans."[4] In listing "integrity,
decency, and sound good sense" as the relevant characteristics of
communities, Reagan emphasized characteristics that all communities were expected to possess and omitted discussion of characteristics that vary across localities: financial resources and the need
for social services.

The idea that local communities are better suited than the federal
government to meet welfare needs appeared in Reagan's speeches as
early as 1975, when he was preparing for his first unsuccessful bid for
the Republican presidential nomination. In a speech to the Executive
Club in Chicago, Reagan argued: "If there is one area of social policy
that should be at the most local level of government possible, it is
welfare. It should not be nationalized, it should be localized. If Joe
Doaks is using his welfare money to go down to the pool hall and
drink beer and gamble, and the people on his block are paying the bill,
Joe is apt to undergo a change in his lifestyle."[5] In this view, if the
redistribution of welfare dollars from taxpayer to recipient happens
at the local rather than at the national level, recipients are much more
likely to be held accountable for their behavior.

The argument that tax dollars are best spent in the communities
where they are raised plays an important role in justifying the "local-
ization" of social policy. Reagan claimed that the "transfer of spending authority to Washington blurs the difference between wasteful
states and prudent ones, and . . . destroys incentives to economy. . . .
[C]itizens will be called upon to pay in federal taxes and inflation for
other states that don't curb their spending." To stress the inherent

unfairness of people's tax dollars going to help those other than themselves, Reagan continued: "The simple fact is the producing class in this nation is being drained of its substance by the non-producers—the taxpayers are being victimized by the tax consumers."

Missing from Reagan's account of why local communities are best suited to meet the social welfare needs of their own residents is the fact that people who need looking after are not uniformly distributed among localities. Reagan's conception of the power and benevolence of local communities seemed to rely on a picture of localities as smaller versions of the national community: composed of some upper- and middle-class residents who will be helping and monitoring some poor residents. As the census data presented in chapter 3 reveal, however, most communities do not mirror the demographic profile of the nation.

Acknowledging the gap between rich and poor communities in the United States reveals that the story of Joe Doaks, who is forced by vigilant neighbors to work rather than collect welfare, is not the full story. If Joe Doaks is dependent on the resources of the people on his block for his welfare payment, that payment is not likely to be very big, because it is highly probable that his neighbors are also poor. But even if his neighbors could afford to ensure that he received a generous welfare payment, their reluctance to encourage the in-migration of other welfare recipients from neighboring towns is also likely to ensure that benefit levels are not high—which brings up the question of mobility.

At the end of his Executive Club speech, Reagan invoked the mobility of the population as another reason why local policy is better policy: "Successful programs and good local governments will attract bright people like magnets, because the genius of federalism is that people can vote with their feet. If local or state governments grow tyrannical and costly, the people will move." Again, Reagan offered a particular view of the local community and its desire to satisfy the preferences of residents. In doing so, he invoked Tiebout's argument that it is more efficient to have large numbers of local governments, offering varied packages of taxes and services, among which residents choose by moving to the community that offers their ideal combination.[6] However, this positive view of the results of competition for residents, which communities engage in by offering a variety of tax and spending packages, assumes that all people are equally attractive as residents. Whereas in fact, people with substantial personal resources and few needs are much more attractive as residents than poor or working-class people.

Political scientists such as Paul Peterson have demonstrated how the desire to attract and retain the most desirable residents ensures that states and localities keep their social welfare efforts at a low level.[7] No community wants to offer welfare benefits generous enough to attract more poor people—or taxes high enough to drive away middle- and upper-income people.

While Reagan did not succeed in achieving a wholesale restructuring of the federal system, he brought to the forefront of the American political consciousness the question of each level of government's appropriate role in that system. What is important for the purposes of this chapter is to see how his arguments invoked a particular conception of local communities and the responsibilities of their residents. Within the context of Reagan's vision, a discussion of social policy invoked not only race and class but location. Depending on where you lived, Reagan's view of the strength of American communities would be more or less accurate—and would define for whose social welfare needs you bore some responsibility.

The Suburban Appeal of Devolution

To suburban dwellers, the appeal of returning federal power to states and localities is that it allows communities with relatively healthy tax bases and relatively few needy residents to keep taxes low and services high. In the words of Robert Reich, "the shift in responsibility for public services to cities and towns has functioned as another means of relieving wealthier Americans of the cost of aiding less fortunate citizens."[8] Similarly, the argument that it is both fairer and more efficient for local communities to take charge of welfare appeals to suburban voters by suggesting, on the one hand, that benevolence is possible, while ensuring, on the other hand, that it won't cost very much. In the words of Thomas Byrne Edsall and Mary D. Edsall, middle-class voters discover "that they can become fiscal liberals at the local level . . . guaranteeing the highest possible return to themselves on their tax dollars, while continuing to maintain policies of fiscal conservatism at the federal level."[9]

In a system where communities use their own resources to look after the needs of their residents, members of suburban communities benefit because they have plentiful resources and few needs. On the other hand, in a system in which the needs of people around the nation are met by the federal government and national tax dollars, residents of predominantly middle- and upper-class areas see their tax dollars leave the community to aid those who live in poorer areas.

The force of the idea that tax dollars somehow "belong" to the community where the taxpayers live shows itself in a number of ways. For one thing, this notion has played a powerful role in the incorporation campaigns of new cities—many of which are essentially suburban areas that acquire city status.[10] For example, the campaign literature used during the fight for the incorporation of Santa Clarita, a predominantly white and upper-middle-class area of Los Angeles County, stressed the need to stop the county's "unfair" taking of tax dollars from Santa Clarita residents in order to meet the needs of large numbers of poor and immigrant residents. In addition, as documented by Evan McKenzie in *Privatopia: Homeowner Associations and the Rise of Residential Private Government,* the desire to keep local resources within the community has played a part in the new politics of homeowners' associations. Residents who pay fees to such associations have argued that they should not have to pay taxes for services that they no longer need the government to provide.[11]

Another Republican position that has strong appeal to suburban dwellers is the support for local autonomy. As a number of researchers have documented, leaving local governments alone to make land-use and zoning decisions ensures that exclusive communities will remain exclusive and that the poor will continue to live in the communities that are unable to exclude them.[12] The difficulty of forming coalitions in support of some forms of metropolitan governance illustrates how reluctant suburban governments are to relinquish these powers of local control, even when suburbanites are not much better off than residents of the nearby city.[13]

Democrats and the Suburban Vote

Clinton's effort to break the Republican lock on the White House by presenting himself as a centrist "new" Democrat has been well documented.[14] What is worth noting, however, is the extent to which this "center" was conceived of as a suburban center: policies were formulated to appeal not just to the middle class but to a specifically suburban middle class.

Before the 1992 presidential election, a number of observers argued that the Democratic Party needed to distance itself from its image as the party of special interests and instead adopt positions that would appeal to the disillusioned middle class.[15] This recommendation was given an explicitly suburban twist by William Schneider, who argued in the *Atlantic Monthly* that to win the 1992 election, the Democratic Party should pursue a suburban strategy—one that appealed to people who "move out to the suburbs . . . to be able to buy their own government" and "resent it when politicians take their money and use it to solve other people's problems." Schneider concluded that "the message to Democrats is: In order to compete for a suburban electorate, keep spending as broad as possible and make taxes as specific as possible."[16]

A number of accounts of the 1992 and 1996 campaigns confirm that Clinton campaign strategists conceived of the voters that they needed to attract as suburban voters: the strategists repeatedly referred to their target voters as suburbanites and explained their technique of polling in shopping malls as an attempt to understand the views of these important suburban voters.[17]

Descriptions of the Democrats' attempt to win back the Reagan Democrats—long-term Democrat identifiers who voted for Reagan in the 1980s—offer further evidence of the extent to which the Democrats in 1992 thought of the electorate in terms of suburban voters. To help the Democratic Party understand the defection of these voters, Stanley Greenberg (who went on to become the pollster for the Clinton campaign), interviewed residents of suburban Macomb County, in Michigan, a place that was viewed as embodying the Reagan Democrat phenomenon. These disillusioned voters felt that the Democratic Party had ignored their interests during the 1980s; on the basis of his discussions with them, Greenberg argued that in order to win the presidency, a Democratic candidate would need to adopt a platform that placed middle-class concerns at the top of the agenda.

Greenberg's report of the Macomb County critique of the Democratic Party makes clear the extent to which the definition of middle-class values and interests is predicated on living in a suburb that keeps residents geographically separated from minorities and the poor.[18] For these suburban middle-class voters, the problem with the Democratic Party was that it spent too much money on too many programs, but Greenberg suggests that this was less a question of "fiscal responsibility and more one of identity of interests." The problem with

Democratic spending was that it was seen as being for the exclusive benefit of minorities.

> These white defectors from the Democratic Party expressed a profound distaste for black Americans, a sentiment that pervaded almost everything they thought about government and politics. Blacks constituted the explanation for their vulnerability and for almost everything that had gone wrong in their lives; not being black was what constituted being middle class; not living with blacks was what made a neighborhood a decent place to live.

For these Reagan Democrats, physical separation from African Americans was central to their sense of middle-class self and their sense that their interests had nothing in common with those of African Americans. In addition, this separation—on the basis of both geography and interests—was clearly identified with the difference between living in the city and living in the suburbs.

> For these white suburban residents, the terms *blacks* and *Detroit* were interchangeable. The city was a place to be avoided—where the kids could not go, where the car got stolen, and where vacant lots and dissolution have replaced their old neighborhoods. . . . These suburban voters felt nothing in common with Detroit and its people and rejected out of hand the social-justice claims of black Americans.

From this sense that the residents of cities were undeserving—yet were awarded advantages in the public policy process—suburban dwellers came to view government as the problem, not the solution, a perspective that Reagan used effectively during his presidential campaign.

> Government to them was more a burden than an ally in their time of trouble. . . . [N]ot one Macomb participant in these discussions could identify an appreciable benefit from government spending or, more pointedly, any benefit from the government's handling of their tax dollars. . . . They strongly suspected that the money was squandered, first and foremost in Detroit. . . . "Why aren't our leaders thinking about all of us?" one man asked. "Detroit is not the state of Michigan. Michigan is a lot bigger than just Detroit."

Greenberg held that understanding the source of the Reagan Democrats' disillusionment could be used to rebuild a winning, bottom-up coalition in support of the Democratic Party. Building this coalition might mean that the Democratic candidate would focus on the middle class in his speeches and policy proposals, but this approach would ultimately benefit the working class and the poor, who want essentially the same things: "A politics grounded in the neighborhoods and families of America will, as a matter of course, promote work and discourage welfare; it will abhor criminality and the breakdown of families; it will accept as common sense tough measures to jail criminals and prevent crime. These are universal instincts that unite black and white and allow Democrats to identify with the values and interests of bottom-up America."

Despite Greenberg's optimism, it is not clear that focusing on issues that would dispel the middle-class fear that the Democratic Party represented only blacks, the cities, and the poor actually resulted in policies that also helped the neediest segments of the population. Geography's role in the formulation and success of policy proposals offers a partial explanation of this result.

In its attempt to attract the suburban middle class in the 1990s, the Democratic Party not only took certain national problems and possible solutions off the table but also moved in the direction of the Republican Party in its critique of federal power and in its celebration of state and local government alternatives. Such support for devolving power away from the national government might—as Greenberg suggested—have resulted in policies that united white, black, poor, working-class, and middle-class Americans, if local communities included representatives from all these groups. However, to the extent that communities today are divided along precisely these lines—and, as Greenberg's Macomb residents illustrate, see their interests as being diametrically opposed—then devolution is likely to hurt poor city dwellers at the expense of middle-class suburbanites.

The discussion that follows illustrates in greater detail how the Democrats' attempt to win back the suburban middle class changed the parameters of the political debate.

Party Platforms and Devolution

The changing language of party platforms from the 1980s, when Reagan won two presidential elections, until 1996, when Clinton became the first Democrat since Roosevelt to win reelection—illustrates how the desire to gain the support of the suburban middle class affected both parties. Conceptions about local communities—what they are like, what they are good at, and what they need—infuse many aspects of policy for both Democrats and Republicans. Particularly during the Reagan years, the contrast between the Republican and Democratic conceptions of local communities was quite clear, but as the Democrats fought to present a message that could win back suburban whites to the party's presidential candidates, the differences between the two parties narrowed.

In 1968, in the aftermath of serious riots in a number of large central cities, the platforms of both political parties strongly emphasized what the Republican platform called "the crisis of the cities." By 1972, however, the Republican platform had clearly shifted its focus toward the concerns of suburban residents. Not only was there no section devoted explicitly to cities, but the platform went out of its way to assure suburban supporters that the Republican Party had no interest in any federal solutions to urban ills that would threaten the sanctity of suburban zoning laws. Instead, the platform supported "locally designed, locally implemented, locally controlled solutions to the problems of individual urban areas," and stated the Republicans' opposition to "the use of housing or community development programs to impose arbitrary housing patterns on unwilling communities."[19] Michael Danielson, in *The Politics of Exclusion,* has vividly documented how, in order to shore up the growing Republican base in the suburbs, Richard Nixon failed to support programs that had been proposed by his secretary of Housing and Urban Development (HUD) which would have required suburbia to participate in desegregation and the creation of low-income housing.[20]

By 1980, with Ronald Reagan the party's nominee for president, the Republican platform reflected an agenda that was not only friendly to the suburban middle class but that was more strongly pro-local and antigovernment in its rhetoric than previous platforms had been. According to the platform, "the Republican Party reaffirms its belief in the decentralization of the federal government and in the traditional American principle that the best government is the one closest to the people. There, it is less costly, more accountable, and more responsive to people's needs."[21]

The particularly suburban appeal of decentralization becomes clear as the platform elaborates further: regional approaches to public policy issues will not be supported because "the regionalization of government encouraged by federal policies diminishes the responsiveness of state and local governments and impairs the power of the people to control their destiny." Decentralization also means doing away with HUD programs that "often infringe upon the right of local government to retain jurisdiction over their own zoning laws and building codes." In keeping with the idea that community boundaries are not to be crossed for public policy purposes, the platform promises not only that local and state governments can manage their own school systems but also strongly opposes "the forced busing of school children to achieve arbitrary racial quotas."

In discussing the problems of the poor in general and cities in particular, the Republican platform stresses the desirability of letting localities take care of their own: "We oppose federalizing the welfare system; local levels of government are most aware of the needs in their communities. We support a block grant program that will help return control of welfare programs to the states. Decisions about who gets welfare, and how much, can be better made on the local level." According to the platform, while Democrats "have proposed more social and fiscal tinkering with our cities and towns," Republicans recognize that it is people helping themselves and their neighbors that offers the best hope for troubled communities. "The American ethic of neighbor helping neighbor has been an essential factor in the building of our nation. Republicans are committed to the preservation of this great tradition."

The Republicans' 1984 platform was written in much the same vein: localities are best equipped to solve the problems of their residents. The federal government should get out of the way because it does more harm than good. "By centralizing responsibility for social programs in Washington, liberal experimenters destroyed the sense of community that sustains local institutions."[22] The message that welfare should not be a federal responsibility was reaffirmed: "Federal administration of welfare is the worst possible, detached from community needs and careless with the public's money." In addition, all "non-essential federal functions should be returned to the states and localities," which "have the capability, knowledge, and sensitivity to local needs" and whose "diverse problems require local understanding."

In 1984 the Republican Party also explicitly addressed the fact that the platform lacked a section devoted solely to the problems of cities.

For far too long, the poor have been trapped by the policies of the Democratic Party which treat those in the ghetto as if their interests were somehow different from our own. That is unfair to us all and an insult to the needy. Their goals are ours; their aspirations we share. To emphasize our common bond, we have addressed their needs in virtually every section of this Platform, rather than segregating them in a token plank. To those who would see the Republican future for urban America, and for those who deserve a better break, we offer the commitments that make up the sinew of this platform.

According to this argument (which sounds similar to the argument that prominent Democrats now make when they urge the party to focus on the middle class), city dwellers are no different from other Americans in their aspirations for freedom and prosperity, goals that are best realized by reducing the federal government's role in people's lives. Accordingly, the platform stated that "renewing the federal system, strengthening the States, and returning power to the people. That is the surest course to our common goal: a free and just society."

Given this line of reasoning, a list of federal initiatives to solve urban ills would be completely counterproductive, since it is the very interference of national government in local areas that is the root cause of so many of today's problems. While the platform extolled the commonality of goals and the virtue of local solutions, regardless of where voters lived, at no time did it address—or even mention—the fact that communities have unequal resources for implementing solutions and realizing goals.

During the decade when Reagan won both presidential elections, the Democrats, for their part, continued to extol the necessity and value of national government action. According to the 1980 platform, Democrats "do not claim that government has all the answers to our problems, but we do believe that government has a legitimate role to play in searching for those answers and in applying those answers."[23] In particular, the Democratic platform argued that reductions in the federal government must not occur at the expense of the poor. Consequently, "spending restraint must be sensitive to those who look to the federal government for aid and assistance, especially to our nation's workers in time of high unemployment," and there must be no "reductions in the funding of any program whose purpose is to serve the basic human needs of the most needy in our society."

While the Republican platform did not discuss the varying resources of local communities, the 1980 Democratic platform made
such disparities central to an argument in favor of a continued
national role in social policy. Under the heading "Targeting and
Regional Balance," the Democrats noted that "from the time of
Franklin Roosevelt, the Democratic Party has dedicated itself to the
principle that the federal government has a duty to ensure that all
regions, states and localities share in the benefits of national economic
prosperity and that none bears more than its share of economic
adversity. . . . To restore balance, national economic policy should be
designed to target federal resources in areas of greatest need."

The Democrats made this same argument—that the varying resources of localities necessitate the involvement of the federal government in ensuring equal access to social goods— in their discussion
of education policy. The Democrats supported an increased federal
role in financing education because such aid "plays a significant role
in guaranteeing that jurisdictions of differing financial capacity can
spend equal amounts on schooling." In addition, in a way that was
sure to be threatening to suburban exclusivity, the platform went on
to state that the "Democratic Party continues to support programs
aimed at achieving communities integrated both in terms of race and
economic class."

Nowhere are the differences in approach between the Democrats
and Republicans more clear than on the topic of welfare. As already
discussed, the Republican platforms of the 1980s called forcefully for
a return of welfare responsibility to states and localities. The Democrats, on the other hand, "strongly rejected" the Republican proposal

> to transfer the responsibility for funding welfare costs entirely to
> the states. Such a proposal would not only worsen the fiscal situ-
> ation of state and local governments, but would also lead to
> reduced benefits and services to those dependent on welfare pro-
> grams. The Democratic policy is exactly the opposite—to provide
> greater assistance to state and local governments for their welfare
> costs and to improve benefits and services for those dependent on
> welfare.

In the Democrats' view, the federal government must help states and
localities meet the needs of their poorest residents precisely because

"these problems are national in scope and require a unified, national response."

Despite the Democrats' failure to win the presidency in 1980, the 1984 platform retained essentially the same features—and contrasts with the Republican platform—as the previous one. Although the message was made less forcibly than it had been in 1980, the platform still clearly called for an active federal government to deal with the myriad challenges facing the nation, and justified this approach largely on the basis of inequalities at lower levels of government. In the realm of jobs and training, because "prosperity will not be evenly distributed among regions and communities ... it is a national responsibility to ensure that the burdens of change are fairly shared."[24] Similarly, in discussions of education, housing, and the hungry and the homeless, the argument was made that a "national effort" was needed. In addition, in marked contrast to the Republican view that city residents would be helped by the same policies that would help everyone else, the Democrats argued for a federal urban policy: "The Democratic Party believes in making our cities' needs a federal priority once again." Such a shift in policy is necessary "because no plan for economic strength will survive when our cities are left behind."

In 1988, in an attempt to shed its image as the party held captive by special interests whose particular needs were catered to in policy prescription after policy prescription, the Democratic Party severely curtailed its platform. Clearly, this alone was not enough to persuade voters to return to the Democratic Party, and in 1992 a full-length platform was reinstated.

This time, however, the message was in clear contrast to that of earlier Democratic platforms: gone was the expansive vision of what the federal government could accomplish; also missing were the arguments about why some public problems required a national approach. The Republicans continued to accuse the Democrats of favoring big-government solutions, but a look at the 1992 Democratic platform (not to mention Clinton's campaign speeches) showed that this charge was no longer accurate.

The 1992 Democratic platform stressed the needs of the middle class and the importance of personal responsibility. While the Democrats still proposed national government programs, the language used to justify these programs had changed. To simultaneously distance themselves from the party's past reputation and distinguish themselves from the Republicans, the Democrats argued for a new ap-

proach to governance that was neither "the Republican proposition
that government has no role nor the old notion that there's a program
for every problem."[25] The Democrats seemed to join in the Republicans' long-standing call to decentralize government, promising "to
take power away from entrenched bureaucracies and narrow interests
in Washington and put it back in the hands of ordinary people. We
vow to make government more decentralized, more flexible and more
accountable."

In a section of the platform entitled "Restoring Community," the
Democrats used language that echoed almost word-for-word a passage in the Republican platform of 1984:

> The success of democracy in America depends substantially on
> the strength of our community institutions: families and neighbor-
> hoods, public schools, religious institutions, charitable organiza-
> tions, civic groups and other voluntary associations. In these social
> networks, the values and character of our citizens are formed as
> we learn the habits and skills of self-government and acquire an
> understanding of our common rights and responsibilities as citi-
> zens. . . . Our communities form a vital "third sector" that lies
> between government and the marketplace. The wisdom, energy
> and resources required to solve our problems are not concen-
> trated in Washington but can be found throughout our communi-
> ties. . . . Government's best role is to enable people and
> communities to solve their own problems.

Both this Tocquevillean message—that citizens learn about self-gov-
ernment through activity in their community—and an anti–big government message—that these communities are best equipped to solve
the problems of their residents—had been present in the 1984 Republican platform:

> America was built on the institutions of home, family, religion,
> and neighborhood. From these basic building blocks came
> self-reliant individuals, prepared to exercise both rights and
> responsibilities.
>
> In the community of individuals and families, every genera-
> tion has relearned the art of self-government. In our neigh-
> borhoods, Americans have traditionally taken care of their needs
> and aided the less fortunate. In the process we developed, inde-

pendent of government, the remarkable network of "mediating institutions"—religious groups, unions, community, and professional associations.[26]

Nevertheless, there are differences between the Democratic and Republican messages. While the Republicans went on to argue that federal programs destroyed the ability of communities to take care of themselves, the Democrats leave open the possibility of some government action by claiming that government can enable communities to help themselves. However, clearly missing is the earlier Democratic critique of the Republican notion that communities are in the best position to take care of their own—namely, that there are vast disparities in communities' access to resources for solving problems.

In discussing the importance of strong community institutions, the Democrats in 1992 criticized the Republicans for urging "Americans to turn inward, to pursue private interest without regard to public responsibilities. By playing racial, ethnic and gender-based politics, they have divided us against each other, created an atmosphere of blame, denial and fear, and undone the hard-fought battles for equality and fairness." What this criticism ignored, however, is that earlier Republican platforms had not advocated turning inward to the individual but inward to the local community: instead of turning to the federal government, neighbors and community members can help each other. What the Democrats—with their own at least partial embrace of this idea—could no longer afford to admit is that when communities are divided along race and class lines, a politics that romanticizes "communities taking care of their own" can also become a politics of division along race and class lines.

The 1996 platforms reflected much the same approach as those of 1992. The Republicans continued to claim that the Democrats favored big-government programs, while they alone believed that "it is government close to home, controlled by neighborhood and community leaders, that can best respond to the needs and values of all citizens."[27] Meanwhile, the Democrats argued that they had "worked hard over the last four years to rein in big government, slash burdensome regulations, eliminate wasteful programs, and shift problem-solving out of Washington and back to people and communities who understand their situations best."[28] The Democrats then went on to claim that they had actually done a better job than the Republicans at realizing longtime Republican promises: "For years, Republicans talked about making government smaller while letting it grow—Democrats are doing it. . . . For years, Republicans talked about shifting power back to states and communities—Democrats are doing it."[29]

In fact, four years of a Democratic presidency had ended with changes in welfare responsibility that corresponded to the unrealized goals of Ronald Reagan in the 1980s. Welfare would no longer be a federal entitlement. Instead, block grants from Washington turned responsibility for meeting welfare needs back to the state governments. While this devolution of responsibility for welfare undoubtedly helped bolster the Democratic claim of having done more than the Republicans to decentralize government, the section of the 1996 platform that deals explicitly with welfare reform seems to reveal some anxiety about the shift. "States asked for this responsibility—now we have to make sure they shoulder it."[30]

The Democrats then proceeded to offer recommendations to states and the business community about what each would need to do to make welfare reform work. While the Republicans continued to argue that only "in the hands of state and local officials, and under the eye of local taxpayers, [can] welfare . . . again become a hand up instead of a handout," the Democrats' discussion of welfare reform does not invoke the argument—which appears elsewhere in the platform—that government closest to the people is best able to meet their needs. The policy consequence in this instance, however, was the same. The Democrats' adoption of a small-government rhetoric meant that they could no longer use arguments about the disparate resources of states and localities to justify a national commitment to welfare provision.[31]

Conclusion

This chapter has explored the connection between presidential party politics and the location of voters. As previous analyses in this volume have shown, and as Greenberg's interviews with the Macomb County suburbanites underscore, the preferences of the suburban middle class cannot be understood without considering the way in which where they live—in addition to their other characteristics—shapes their political understanding and preferences.

The Democratic move to the center must also be understood as a move to the suburban center. Democrats clearly saw the voters whom they needed to attract as suburban dwellers and as Reagan voters, and felt that in order to succeed they needed to offer a vision of smaller, less national government.

Finally, the Republican—and, increasingly, the Democratic argument—about the desirability of small government must also be considered in light of what is known about where people live. A politics that calls for the return of social programs to state and local governments introduces a place-specific dimension into policies that are not necessarily about place. In addition, it is likely to have greater appeal to people who live in prosperous communities with few needs and many resources than to people who live in communities with many needs and few resources.

Notes

1. See, for example, E. J. Dionne Jr., *Why Americans Hate Politics* (New York: Simon and Schuster), 1991; Thomas Byrne Edsall and Mary D. Edsall, *Chain Reaction: The Impact of Race, Rights, and Taxes on American Politics* (New York: W.W. Norton, 1992); Stanley B. Greenberg, *Middle Class Dreams: The Politics and Power of the New American Majority* (New York: Times Books, 1995).

2. Although Nixon also advocated policies that he referred to collectively as "new federalism," these policies differed significantly from those embodied in Reagan's version of federalism. One example of the differences is the fact that Reagan ended general revenue sharing, one of the important components of Nixon's new federalism. For a comparison of Nixon's and Reagan's federalism, see Timothy Conlan, *New Federalism: Intergovernmental Reform from Nixon to Reagan* (Washington, D.C.: Brookings Institution Press, 1988).

3. Ronald Reagan, *Public Papers of the Presidents of the United States: Ronald Reagan, 1982,* vol. I (Washington, D.C.: GPO, 1982), 72–78.

4. Ibid.

5. Quotations from Reagan's speech to the Executive Club are from the *Congressional Record,* 94th Cong., 1st sess., 1975, 121, pt. 24:31184–31186.

6. Charles Tiebout, "A Pure Theory of Local Expenditures," *Journal of Political Economy* 64, no. 4 (October 1956). See also James M. Buchanan, "Principles of Urban Fiscal Strategy," *Public Choice* 4 (fall 1971); Thomas Dye, *American Federalism: Competition among Governments* (Lexington, Mass.: D.C. Heath, 1990).

7. Paul E. Peterson, *City Limits* (Chicago: University of Chicago Press, 1981); Paul E. Peterson and Mark C. Rom, *Welfare Magnets: A New Case for a National Standard* (Washington, D.C.: Brookings Institution Press, 1988).

8. Robert B. Reich, "Succession of the Successful," *New York Times Magazine,* 20 January 1991.

9. Edsall and Edsall, *Chain Reaction,* 228.

10. B. Drummond Ayres Jr., "Los Angeles, Long-Fragmented, Faces Threat of Secession by the San Fernando Valley," *New York Times,* 29 May 1996, p. A12; Nancy Burns, *The Formation of American Local Governments: Private Values in Public Institutions* (New York: Oxford University Press, 1994); Gary Miller, *Cities by Contract: The Politics of Municipal Incorporation* (Cambridge, Mass.: MIT Press, 1981).

11. Evan Mackenzie, *Privatopia: Homeowner Associations and the Rise of Residential Private Government* (New Haven, Conn.: Yale University Press, 1994), 164–66.

12. Richard Briffault, "Localism and Legal Theory (Our Localism, Part 2)," *Columbia Law Review* 90, no. 2 (March 1990); Michael D. Danielson, *The Politics of Exclusion* (New York: Columbia University Press, 1976).

13. Myron Orfield, *Metropolitics: A Regional Agenda for Community and Stability* (Washington, D.C.: Brookings Institution Press; Cambridge, Mass.: Lincoln Institute of Land Policy, 1997).

14. Elizabeth Drew, *Showdown: The Struggle between the Gingrich Congress and the Clinton White House* (New York: Simon and Schuster, 1996); Dick Morris, *Behind the Oval Office: Winning the Presidency in the 1990s* (New York: Random House, 1997); Evan Thomas et al., *Back From the Dead: How Clinton Survived the Republican Revolution* (New York: Atlantic Monthly Press, 1997).

15. Dionne, *Why Americans Hate Politics;* Edsall and Edsall, *Chain Reaction;* William Schneider, "The Suburban Century Begins: The Real Meaning of the 1992 Election," *Atlantic Monthly,* July 1992.

16. Schneider, "Suburban Century," 37, 39.

17. Michael Kranish and Brian McGrory, "Suburbs Are Key in Clinton Election Plan," *Boston Globe,* 1 September 1996, p. A1; Morris, *Behind the Oval Office;* Thomas et al., *Back From the Dead;* Bob Woodward, *The Agenda* (New York: Simon and Schuster, 1994).

18. The question arises to what extent the views of Macomb County citizens are representative of those of other swing voters. What matters here is that Greenberg believed that they were, and advised the Democratic Party accordingly. In a footnote, he remarks that "the 'Macomb state of mind' is probably evident among many of those who have moved into politically volatile, rapid growth suburban areas." Quotations in the text from Greenberg, *Middle Class Dreams,* are from pp. 297, 39, 43, and 284.

19. Donald Bruce Johnson, ed., *National Party Platforms, Volume II, 1960–1976.* (Urbana: University of Illinois Press, 1978).

20. Danielson, *Politics of Exclusion.*

21. Quotations in the text from the 1980 Republican platform are from the *Congressional Quarterly Almanac 1980* (Washington, D.C.: CQ Press, 1980), 71B, 66B, 63B, 60B, and 64-65B.

22. Quotations in the text from the 1984 Republican platform are from the *Congressional Quarterly Almanac 1984* (Washington, D.C.: CQ Press, 1984), 46B, 47B, 55B, and 52B.

23. Quotations in the text from the 1980 Democratic platform are from the *Congressional Quarterly Almanac 1980* (Washington, D.C.: CQ Press, 1992), 96B, 92B, 93B, 100B, and 99B.

24. Quotations in the text from the 1984 Democratic platform are from the *Congressional Quarterly Almanac 1984* (Washington, D.C.: CQ Press, 1992), 81B, 80B, 82B, 96B, and 81B.

25. Quotations from the 1992 Democratic platform are from the *Congressional Quarterly Almanac 1992* (Washington, D.C.: CQ Press, 1992), 59A and 62A.

26. *Congressional Quarterly Almanac 1984,* 46B.

27. *Congressional Quarterly Weekly Report,* 17 August 1996, 2321.

28. Ibid., *Democratic Convention Supplement,* 43.

29. Ibid.

30. Ibid., 42.

31. Given that the argument here is primarily about the role of communities in the program of the two parties, it is important to note the role that communities play in a system that devolves welfare responsibility back to the states. Under the Aid to Families with Dependent Children program, some states had already required localities to bear part of the cost of welfare, and new welfare plans in some states may involve an even greater role for local government. A report in the *New York Times* on the initial impact of welfare reform found that "some states have considered letting individual counties set time limits of their own. Republicans in Colorado pushed such a plan, but they were thwarted by the state's Democratic governor, Roy Romer. Critics of such local autonomy worry that localities will abuse it to drive poor families away. In Colorado, skeptics issued a warning: Welfare reform is not a bus ticket to Denver" (Jason DeParle, "U.S. Welfare System Dies As State Programs Emerge," *New York Times,* 30 June 1997, p. A11.) In analyses of the devolution of responsibilities from the national government to states, researchers have frequently described the tendency of state governments to "pass the buck" to local governments with few resources. See, for example, Margaret Weir, "Is Anybody Listening? The Uncertain Future of Welfare Reform in the Cities," *Brookings Review* 15, no. 1 (winter 1997).

CHAPTER NINE

Prospects for the Future

Contemporary American politics are fundamentally shaped by the geographic sorting of voters along racial and economic lines. People with similar socioeconomic characteristics who live in different kinds of communities have different political preferences. Compared with their urban counterparts, suburban dwellers are more likely to identify as Republicans and vote for Republican candidates, and less likely to support federal government spending, particularly on redistributive programs. The more racially and economically homogeneous the suburban area, and the more the suburban area differs from the nearby city, the stronger the relationship between location and distinctive political attitudes.

As the suburbs become home to an increasing proportion of the national electorate, the distinctive preferences of suburbanites shape American politics in particular ways, two of which are detailed in this volume. First, in a system that is based on geographic representation, the clustering of like-minded voters in particular locations finds easy expression in the political system. A look at the contemporary Congress illustrates how this occurs: while the numbers of urban, rural, and mixed districts have declined since the 1970s, the number of predominantly suburban districts has increased significantly. And as the percentage of the district's population that is suburban increases, the district is increasingly likely to be represented in Congress by a Republican, and the Democratic proportion of the vote declines: that is, the district becomes an increasingly safe Republican seat.

Second, the political messages of the two parties have increasingly been designed to appeal to these majority suburban voters. Consequently, the Democratic Party has joined the Republican Party in calling for a smaller federal government and the devolution of social programs to the state and local levels. This approach to social policy is attractive to suburban voters, who view their move to the suburbs as a means of escaping the problems of the urban poor and the high costs of solving them. Devolution is more appealing to those who live in communities with many resources and few needs (predominantly the suburbs) than to those living in communities with few resources and many needs (predominantly the cities). In its quest to attract the suburban voter, the Democratic Party removed from its 1996 party platform any reference to the fact that there are disparities between the needs and resources of different kinds of localities.

What, then, are the prospects for an increased federal role in solving the problems of cities and the poor, given the continuing growth of the suburban population? The implications of the findings presented here are mixed. As older suburbs come to experience some of the problems usually associated with cities, their residents can be expected to become more supportive of spending on federal programs and less supportive of the Republican Party. This expectation is the basis for the optimistic views of some urban scholars who believe that the cities will not be left to die: as suburban residents experience problems similar to those found in cities, a group powerful enough to push for government involvement in solving these problems will come into being. Statistical analysis may already have demonstrated the interconnectedness of urban and suburban areas, but much more persuasive for suburban residents will be the experience of city-type woes in their own backyards.[1]

Nevertheless, this interpretation of the impact of increasing racial and economic diversity in the suburbs is not the only possible one. First, the findings presented here also demonstrate that city and suburban residents do not respond in the same ways to a shared metropolitan environment. To the extent that suburbs and cities within the same metropolitan area continue to be home to very different populations, suburban residents are likely to continue to pursue a strategy of lowered support for federal spending and increased support for the political party that favors devolution of power to the state and local levels. In other words, they will support whichever policies and candidates will allow their tax dollars to stay within the suburbs instead of disappearing to pay for expensive and difficult solutions to problems primarily located in the cities. If decline in suburban areas is accompanied by even more severe decline in the central city, the reaction of the suburban dwellers may not be at all conducive to the formation of city-suburb coalitions to push the federal and state governments for solutions to urban ills.

Second, even as the degree of city-suburb disparity declines, the findings presented here also demonstrate that people sometimes respond to a common threat with a desire to separate themselves from others rather than with recognition of a shared interest. Beginning signs of decline in their own localities seem to make people even less supportive of policies that they view as being beneficial to groups other than themselves—the "undeserving" poor. Thus, the possibilities for building coalitions across the city-suburban divide depend on whether, in the face of similar problems, suburbanites see their fate as linked with those of city residents or see themselves as engaged in a zero-sum game with their urban counterparts. In his analysis of the potential for the formation of city-suburb coalitions, Orfield notes that public officials from declining suburban areas are initially reluctant to see their fates as linked with those of city residents: "At first, the suburbs (no matter how badly off) saw no reason to join in a political alliance with the central cities. Foreign to their worldview, the very idea smacked of a sort of political degradation. In addition, some suburban city officials did not want to publicly acknowledge any problems."[2]

While Orfield is ultimately optimistic about the potential for uniting the central cities and inner-ring suburbs in support of metropolitan-wide tax-base sharing and fair-housing policies, he acknowledges the intensive effort that will be required to build and maintain the coalition with inner suburbs who "are not powerfully disposed to believe that an alliance with their previous enemy is either wise or politically expedient."[3] As long as people remain geographically isolated, the recognition of common interests will be neither easy nor automatic.

Given the growth of the suburban share of the electorate and the difficulties of forming city-suburban coalitions, some political analysts argue that policies intended ultimately to aid the urban poor will succeed only if they are presented in non-place-specific terms designed to appeal to the suburban middle class.[4] The findings presented here, however, suggest that this strategy has drawbacks. First, even if policies are presented in place-neutral terms, support for them will vary with location. Consequently, designing policies to appeal to the suburban middle class will not necessarily yield results that also benefit the urban poor. Voters' preferences are affected in important ways by the communities in which they reside, regardless of whether government policies are presented as benefiting particular kinds of locations.

Second, attempts to attract suburban voters lead both Republicans and Democrats to offer policy alternatives with important place-specific features: for example, discussions of welfare reform invoke the idea of communities helping themselves and their own residents and extol the virtue of policies that are developed and implemented closer to the people they serve. If this political discourse occurs without reference to the disparities in needs and resources among communities, the end result is increasing support for the politics of localism at the precise moment that cities are least able to take care of their own.

This romanticized vision of local communities surfaces not only in discussions of devolving responsibility for social policy but in recent discussions of the need to revitalize political communities in the face of increasing dissatisfaction with government.[5] While strong, vital communities are certainly worth supporting, any discussion of the role that these communities can play in political life must not ignore the reality of division along racial, ethnic, and economic lines that characterizes many localities in America. City residents can organize to improve their own communities, but these initiatives will necessarily be limited.[6] Existing imbalance in the ratio of needs to resources—and the fear of increasing this imbalance by offering policies that attract poor people—will ensure that city assistance to low-income residents remains limited.[7]

One reason that the idea of community is so compelling is that it suggests the recognition of common bonds of obligation and affection. But any real understanding of the importance of community—and any real recognition of common bonds—must cross city-suburb boundaries. In an interesting series of articles, legal scholar Gerald Frug makes precisely this point. Many contemporary discussions of the importance of communities ignore the interconnectedness of those same communities. As citizens cannot be understood outside the context of particular communities, so particular communities cannot be understood outside the context of particular regions.[8]

How, then, can this more expansive understanding of political community be developed in contemporary suburban America? Orfield points to the importance of committed political leaders who are willing to expend the energy and political capital necessary to form coalitions across intrametropolitan boundaries.[9] Intergovernmental bodies—agencies with metropolitan-wide jurisdiction, for example—can create overarching interests even as particular localities remain segregated along lines of class and race, although even here the importance of political leadership in helping create and sustain such overarching governmental agencies is clear.[10] Future research needs, first, to consider the issues that can unite city and suburban residents around common goals; second, it needs to explore strategies that can be used successfully to persuade residents of particular metropolitan areas to see their fates as linked across city-suburb boundaries.

Coalitions in support of redistributive programs will be formed across city-suburb boundaries only as a result of sustained discussions of place that focus on the variations in resources and needs of particular localities. A successful political agenda for urban American requires that the current political debate move beyond romanticized images of the powers of local communities toward a discussion of the interconnectedness of cities, suburbs, and regions. Revitalizing political community is a worthy goal—but only if the community is a community that transcends local government boundaries. Making these connections will be difficult, but the alternative is the continuing balkanization of America.[11]

Notes

1. For discussions of the interconnectedness of cities and suburbs, see Edward W. Hill, Harold L. Wolman, and Coit Cook Ford III, "Can Suburbs Survive without their Central Cities? Examining the Suburban Dependence

Hypothesis," *Urban Affairs Review* 31, no. 2 (November 1995), 147–74; H. V. Savitch et al., "Ties that Bind: Central Cities, Suburbs, and the New Metropolitan Region," *Economic Development Quarterly 7*, no. 4 (November 1993), 341–57.

2. Myron Orfield, *Metropolitics: A Regional Agenda for Community and Stability* (Washington, D.C.: Brookings Institution Press; Cambridge, Mass.: Lincoln Institute of Land Policy, 1997), 108.

3. Ibid., 38.

4. See, for example, E. J. Dionne Jr., *Why Americans Hate Politics* (New York: Simon and Schuster, 1991); Stanley B. Greenberg, *Middle Class Dreams: The Politics and Power of the New American Majority* (New York: Times Books, 1995); Theda Skocpol, "Sustainable Social Policy: Fighting Poverty without Poverty Programs," *American Prospect* 1, no. 2 (summer 1990); Skocpol, "A Partnership with American Families," in *The New Majority: Toward a Popular Progressive Politics*, ed. Stanley B. Greenberg and Theda Skocpol (New Haven, Conn.: Yale University Press, 1997); William Julius Wilson, *When Work Disappears: The World of the New Urban Poor* (New York: Vintage Books, 1997), 183–206.

5. Dionne, *Why Americans Hate Politics*, 329–55; Michael J. Sandel, *Democracy's Discontent: America in Search of a Public Philosophy* (Cambridge, Mass.: Harvard University Press, Belknap Press, 1996).

6. Robert Halpern, *Rebuilding the Inner City: A History of Neighborhood Initiatives to Address Poverty in the United States* (New York: Columbia University Press, 1995), 219–23.

7. Paul E. Peterson, *City Limits* (Chicago: University of Chicago Press, 1981).

8. Gerald E. Frug, *Citymaking: Building Communities without Building Walls* (Princeton, N.J.: Princeton University Press, 1993), 73–112.

9. Orfield, *Metropolitics*.

10. Anthony Downs, *New Visions for Metropolitan America* (Washington, D.C.: Brookings Institution Press; Cambridge, Mass.: Lincoln Institute of Land Policy, 1994); Frug, *Citymaking;* Orfield, *Metropolitics.*

11. The term *balkanization* was drawn from William H. Frey, "Immigration, Domestic Migration, and Demographic Balkanization in America: New Evidence for the 1990s," *Population and Development Review* 22, no. 4 (December 1996).

Appendix—Tables

Table 1. Socioeconomic Characteristics of Suburban and City Residents, 1990

Characteristic	Suburbs	Cities	Difference (cities − suburbs)
High school education	80.8	73.0	7.8
Bachelor's degree	24.6	21.9	2.7
Children in two-parent families	76.8	59.8	17.0
Unemployed	5.0	7.8	2.8
Persons in poverty	7.8	18.0	10.2
Families in poverty	5.7	14.1	8.4
Owner-occupied housing	67.8	49.0	18.8
Median household income ($)	37,007	26,727	10,280
Per capita income ($)	17,097	13,839	3,258

Source: Bureau of the Census, *1990 Census of Population. Social and Economic Characteristics Metropolitan Areas* (Washington, D.C.: GPO, November 1993), tables 1 and 2; Bureau of the Census, *1990 Census of Housing; General Housing Characteristics, United States* (Washington, D.C.: GPO, November 1992), table 1.
Note: Figures are percentages unless otherwise noted.

Table 2. Racial and Ethnic Composition of Suburbs and Cities, 1990

Racial or ethnic group	Suburbs %	Cities %	Difference (city − suburb)	Nation %
White	84.8	66.2	17.8	80.3
Non-Hispanic white	80.0	59.2	20.8	75.8
Hispanic	8.5	14.5	6.0	8.8
Black	8.3	22.0	13.7	12.0
Asian	3.7	4.3	0.6	2.9

Source: Bureau of the Census, *1990 Census of Population. Social and Economic Characteristics* (Washington, D.C.: GPO, November 1993), table 4.

Table 3. Socioeconomic Characteristics by Location and Race, 1990

Characteristic	White[a]		Black	
	Suburbs	Cities	Suburbs	Cities
High school education	83.3	80.6	74.1	63.4
Bachelor's degree	25.7	27.0	16.8	10.9
Unemployed	4.3	5.2	9.4	14.4
Persons in poverty	5.8	10.7	18.5	31.1
Families in poverty	4.3	7.8	16.1	28.1
Median household income ($)	38,061	30,204	28,635	18,703
Per capita income ($)	18,490	17,339	11,385	8,713

Source: Bureau of the Census, *1990 Census of Population. Social and Economic Characteristics* (Washington, D.C.: GPO, November 1993), tables 7 and 11.
Note: Figures are percentages unless otherwise noted.
[a]Figures are for the non-Hispanic white population.

Table 4. Suburban and City Commuting Patterns, 1990

Characteristic	Suburbs	Cities
Work in city	29	76
Work in own metro area, but not in city	60	18
Work outside own metro area	11	6
Commute less than 10 minutes	14	14
Commute more than 45 minutes	12	13
Commute on public transit	4	12
Mean commuting time (minutes)	23.5	22.3

Source: Author's calculations from Bureau of the Census, *1990 Census of Population. Social and Economic Characteristics* (Washington, D.C.: GPO, November 1993), table 18.
Note: Figures are percentages unless otherwise noted.

Table 5. Socioeconomic Characteristics by Region, 1990

Characteristic	Northeast Suburbs (%)	Northeast Cities (%)	Midwest Suburbs (%)	Midwest Cities (%)	South Suburbs (%)	South Cities (%)	West Suburbs (%)	West Cities (%)
White	91.6	62.1	93.5	68.8	83.4	64.3	77.9	69.4
Black	5.1	25.0	4.1	25.5	12.6	28.4	4.4	8.4
Asian	1.9	4.5	1.3	2.0	1.6	1.7	7.3	10.0
Hispanic	3.8	16.0	2.0	5.8	6.9	13.2	19.3	22.0
High school education or above	80.5	68.6	81.5	73.6	80.0	73.0	79.8	77.5
Persons in poverty	6.0	18.6	6.5	19.2	10.4	19.1	7.9	14.9
Owner-occupied housing	72.2	39.4	75.1	53.0	71.6	52.0	64.1	49.7

Source: Bureau of the Census, *1990 Census of Population and Housing. Supplementary Reports* (Washington, D.C.: GPO, December 1993), tables 2, 5, 7, and 9.
Notes: Data for regions were available only for whites, not for non-Hispanic whites. In addition, the data were based on definitions of metropolitan areas that were updated as of 30 June 1993. Consequently, while the figures can be compared across regions, they cannot be compared directly with the figures in tables 1 and 2.

Table 6. Socioeconomic Measures: Average Suburb/City Ratios across All Metropolitan Areas, 1990

Characteristic	Suburb/City Ratio
Population density	0.06
Black	0.17
High school education or above	1.02
Bachelor's degree	0.94
Per capita income	1.08
Female-headed households	0.64
Unemployed	0.77
Living in poverty	0.49
Owner-occupied housing	1.41

Source: Author's analysis of Bureau of the Census, *1990 Census of Population and Housing,* summary tape file 3C, 1992.
Note: Ratios were derived from comparisons of percentages, except in the cases of population density and per capita income, which were derived from raw numbers.

Table 7. Party Identification, 1952–1992

Variable	Coefficient	Standard error	T-statistic
Constant	2.87		
Age	.06	.009	7.02
Income	.11	.01	8.03
Education	.16	.01	16.97
Male	.001	.03	.04
African American	−1.38	.05	30.03
Southern	−.38	.03	11.49
Jewish	−1.55	.07	20.69
Catholic	−.76	.03	23.46
Living in a suburb	.23	.08	3.01
Living in a suburb (by time period)			
1960s	.04	.10	.36
1970s	−.09	.09	.92
1980–86	.01	.10	.10
1988–92	.19	.11	1.82
Period of study			
1960s	−.15	.07	2.16
1970s	.08	.06	1.24
1980–86	−.11	.07	1.51
1988–92	−.10	.08	1.27

Source: American National Election Studies Cumulative Data, 1948–1992 (Ann Arbor, Mich.: Inter-University Consortium for Political and Social Research, 1995).
Notes: Table entries are the results of ordinary least squares analysis. Party identification scores were based on a seven-point scale in which 1 = strong Democrat and 7 = strong Republican. $N = 19,052$.

Table 8. Congressional Vote, 1952–1992

Variable	Coefficient	Standard error	T-statistic
Constant	−1.06		
Age	.09	.01	6.20
Income	.17	.02	7.53
Education	.13	.01	8.71
Male	−.03	.04	.75
African American	−1.88	.11	16.56
Southern	−.44	.06	7.90
Jewish	−1.62	.12	13.22
Catholic	−.71	.05	14.75
Living in a suburb	.22	.11	2.09
Living in a suburb (by time period)			
1960s	.07	.14	.53
1970s	−.08	.13	.57
1980–86	.20	.14	1.40
1988–92	.50	.17	3.00
Period of study			
1960s	−.19	.11	1.83
1970s	−.30	.10	2.92
1980–86	−.48	.11	4.22
1988–92	−.90	.14	6.60

Source: American National Election Studies Cumulative Data, 1948–1992 (Ann Arbor, Mich.: Inter-University Consortium for Political and Social Research, 1995).
Notes: Table entries are the results of logit analysis. Positive numbers indicate pro-Republican effects. $N = 10{,}424$.

Table 9. Congressional Vote (with Party Identification), 1952–1992

Variable	Coefficient	Standard error	T-statistic
Party identification	.64	.01	47.95
Living in a suburb	.08	.13	.66
Living in a suburb (by time period)			
1960s	.14	.17	.84
1970s	.03	.16	.16
1980–86	.21	.17	1.22
1988–92	.40	.20	2.03

Source: American National Election Studies Cumulative Data, 1948–1992 (Ann Arbor, Mich.: Inter-University Consortium for Political and Social Research, 1995).
Notes: Table entries are the results of logit analysis. In addition to the variables shown, the following variables were controlled for: age, income, education, gender, race, religion, living in the South, and time period. Positive numbers indicate pro-Republican effects. $N = 10,392$.

Table 10. Presidential Vote, 1954–1992

Variable	Coefficient	Standard error	T-statistic
Constant	−.60		
Age	.11	.02	6.34
Income	.16	.03	5.72
Education	.13	.02	7.11
Male	.09	.05	1.79
African American	−2.56	.14	18.50
Southern	.06	.07	.86
Jewish	−1.89	.14	13.11
Catholic	−.59	.06	10.31
Living in a suburb	.10	.12	.81
Living in a suburb (by time period)			
1960s	.21	.16	1.30
1970s	.11	.16	.65
1980–86	.54	.17	3.08
1988–92	.28	.18	1.53
Period of study			
1960s	−.87	.12	7.30
1970s	−.28	.12	2.30
1980–86	−.59	.14	4.32
1988–92	−.78	.15	5.36

Source: American National Election Studies Cumulative Data, 1948–1992 (Ann Arbor, Mich.: Inter-University Consortium for Political and Social Research, 1995).
Notes: Table entries are the results of logit analysis. Positive numbers indicate pro-Republican effects $N = 7,120$.

Table 11. Presidential Vote (with Party Identification), 1954–1992

Variable	Coefficient	Standard error	T-statistic
Party identification	.85	.02	41.88
Living in a suburb	−.03	.15	.19
Living in a suburb (by time period)			
1960s	.12	.21	.56
1970s	.20	.20	.96
1980–86	.56	.22	2.50
1988–92	.18	.24	.74

Source: American National Election Studies Cumulative Data, 1948–1992 (Ann Arbor, Mich.: Inter-University Consortium for Political and Social Research, 1995).
Notes: Table entries are the results of logit analysis. In addition to the variables shown, the following variables were controlled for: age, income, education, gender, race, religion, living in the South, and time period. Positive numbers indicate pro-Republican effects. $N = 7,091$.

Table 12. Characteristics of National Election Study Respondents, 1988–1992

Characteristics	Suburbs	Cities
Population	64.0	36.0
Mean age (years)	44.5	44.4
Income (percentile)		
0–33	23.7	35.1
34–100	76.4	64.8
Education		
Some college or more	33.9	30.6
Gender		
Male	54.4	52.6
Female	45.6	47.4
Race		
White	90.5	69.6
African American	7.3	27.4

Source: American National Election Studies, 1988, 1990, and 1992 (Ann Arbor, Mich.: Inter-University Consortium for Political and Social Research, 1995).
Note: Figures are percentages unless otherwise noted.

Table 13. Presidential Vote, 1988–1992

Explanatory variable	Coefficient	Standard error	T-statistic
Constant	5.42		
Party identification	−1.03	.06	18.21
Age	−.01	.007	2.26
Income	−.04	.11	.41
Education	−.07	.07	1.06
Male	−.22	.19	1.20
African American	.89	.30	2.91
Southern	−.98	.25	4.00
Catholic	−.16	.20	.80
Jewish	.86	.56	1.56
Suburban	−.19	.20	.93
Homeowner	.08	.23	.35
Married with children	−.18	.22	.82

Source: American National Election Studies, 1988, 1990, and 1992 (Ann Arbor, Mich.: Inter-University Consortium for Political and Social Research, 1995).
Notes: Table entries are the results of logit analysis. Positive numbers indicate pro-Democratic effects. $N = 1,168$. Log-likelihood $= -406.52$.

Table 14. Presidential Vote (Not Controlling for Party Identification), 1988–1992

Explanatory variable	Coefficient	Standard error	T-statistic
Constant	2.12		
Age	−.01	.004	2.41
Income	−.19	.07	2.58
Education	−.18	.05	3.83
Male	−.33	.13	2.53
African American	1.86	.24	7.86
Southern	−.35	.17	2.07
Catholic	.21	.14	1.54
Jewish	1.86	.44	4.23
Suburban	−.39	.14	2.76
Homeowner	.04	.16	.24
Married with children	−.17	.15	1.13

Source: American National Election Studies, 1988, 1990, and 1992 (Ann Arbor, Mich.: Inter-University Consortium for Political and Social Research, 1995).
Notes: Table entries are the results of logit analysis. Positive numbers indicate pro-Democratic effects. $N = 1,173$. Log-likelihood $= -717.5$.

Table 15. Support for Perot, 1992

Explanatory variable	Coefficient	Standard error	T-statistic
Constant	−1.12		
Party identification	.07	.05	1.55
Age	−.02	.006	3.19
Income	.05	.02	2.45
Education	−.11	.04	2.52
Female	−.56	.18	3.09
White	1.68	.48	3.52
Southern	−.18	.20	.91
Catholic	.27	.20	1.36
Jewish	−.03	.58	.02
Suburban	.44	.21	2.10
Homeowner	−.28	.22	1.25
Married with children	−.05	.20	.23

Source: American National Election Studies, 1988, 1990 and 1992 (Ann Arbor, Mich.: Inter-University Consortium for Political and Social Research, 1995).
Notes: Table entries are the results of logit analysis. Positive numbers indicate pro-Perot effects. $N = 997$. Log-likelihood = −414.77.

Table 16. Congressional Vote, 1988–1992

Explanatory variable	Coefficient	Standard error	T-statistic
Constant	3.66		
Party identification	−.66	.04	15.75
Age	−.003	.005	.56
Income	−.17	.09	1.89
Education	−.002	.06	.03
Male	−.09	.15	.61
African American	.57	.30	1.91
Southern	−.04	.21	.22
Catholic	.07	.17	.41
Jewish	.10	.47	.22
Suburban	−.38	.18	2.13
Homeowner	.10	.20	.51
Married with children	−.26	.18	1.43
Democratic incumbent	1.59	.21	7.59
Republican incumbent	−1.37	.24	5.83

Source: American National Election Studies, 1988, 1990 and 1992 (Ann Arbor, Mich.: Inter-University Consortium for Political and Social Research, 1995).
Notes: Table entries are the results of logit analysis. Positive numbers indicate pro-Democratic effects. $N = 1,549$. Log-likelihood = −559.12.

Table 17. Party Identification, 1988–1992

Explanatory variable	Coefficient	Standard error	T-statistic
Constant	5.14		
Age	.004	.002	1.71
Income	−.19	.04	4.78
Education	−.13	.03	5.13
Male	−.17	.07	2.38
African American	1.23	.10	12.35
Southern	.09	.09	.99
Catholic	.35	.08	4.50
Jewish	1.47	.24	6.20
Suburban	−.44	.08	5.70
Homeowner	.17	.08	2.06
Married with children	−.12	.08	1.44

Source: American National Election Studies, 1988, 1990, and 1992 (Ann Arbor, Mich.: Inter-University Consortium for Political and Social Research, 1995).
Notes: Table entries are the results of ordinary least squares analysis. Party identification scores were based on a seven-point scale in which 1 = strong Republican and 7 = strong Democrat. N = 3,060.

Table 18. Support for Aid to Cities, 1992

Explanatory variable	Coefficient	Standard error	T-statistic
Constant	.85		
Party identification	−.11	.02	6.45
Age	.006	.002	3.04
Income	.006	.006	.90
Education	.03	.01	2.07
Female	.13	.06	2.02
White	−.37	.09	4.02
Southern	.19	.07	2.74
Catholic	.03	.07	.45
Jewish	.67	.21	3.17
Suburban	−.23	.07	3.42
Homeowner	−.20	.07	2.68
Married with children	−.15	.07	2.16

Source: American National Election Studies, 1988, 1990, and 1992 (Ann Arbor, Mich.: Inter-University Consortium for Political and Social Research, 1995).
Notes: Table entries are the results of ordered probit analysis. Positive numbers indicate pro-aid effects. N = 1,365. Log-likelihood = −1335.2. Threshold = 1.44.

Table 19. Support for Spending on Programs to Assists Blacks, 1988–1992

Explanatory variable	Coefficient	Standard error	T-statistic
Constant	1.40		
Party identification	−.11	.01	10.05
Age	.002	.001	1.11
Income	−.02	.02	.94
Education	.03	.02	2.10
Male	−.09	.04	2.15
African American	.94	.07	14.24
Southern	.03	.05	.59
Catholic	.05	.05	1.00
Jewish	.04	.15	.25
Suburban	−.16	.05	3.33
Homeowner	−.14	.05	2.72
Married with children	.04	.05	.70

Source: American National Election Studies, 1988, 1990, and 1992 (Ann Arbor, Mich.: Inter-University Consortium for Political and Social Research, 1995).
Notes: Table entries are the results of ordered probit analysis. Positive numbers indicate pro-spending effects. $N = 2,938$. Log-likelihood $= -2639.6$. Threshold $= 1.70$.

Table 20. Support for Government Spending and Services, 1988–1992

Explanatory variable	Coefficient	Standard error	T-statistic
Constant	6.54		
Party identification	−.16	.01	10.91
Age	−.01	.002	6.11
Income	−.10	.03	3.11
Education	−.13	.02	6.26
Male	−.32	.06	5.36
African American	.51	.09	5.87
Southern	−.02	.07	.21
Catholic	.20	.07	3.03
Jewish	.17	.19	.89
Suburban	−.18	.07	2.84
Homeowner	−.17	.07	2.43
Married with children	−.10	.07	1.40

Source: American National Election Studies, 1988, 1990, and 1992 (Ann Arbor, Mich.: Inter-University Consortium for Political and Social Research, 1995).
Notes: Table entries are the results of ordinary least squares analysis. Positive numbers indicate pro-spending effects. $N = 2,592$.

Table 21. Support for Spending on Food Stamps, 1988–1992

Explanatory variable	Coefficient	Standard error	T-statistic
Constant	1.43		
Party identification	−.11	.01	9.88
Age	.0001	.001	.09
Income	−.15	.02	6.22
Education	−.02	.02	1.08
Male	−.07	.04	1.66
African American	.34	.06	5.46
Southern	−.15	.05	2.94
Catholic	−.007	.05	.15
Jewish	.05	.14	.36
Suburban	−.08	.05	1.70
Homeowner	−.22	.05	4.47
Married with children	.008	.05	.15

Source: American National Election Studies, 1988, 1990, and 1992 (Ann Arbor, Mich.: Inter-University Consortium for Political and Social Research, 1995).
Notes: Table entries are the results of ordered probit analysis. Positive numbers indicate pro-spending effects. N = 2,940. Log-likelihood = −2781.3. Threshold = 1.59.

Table 22. Support for Spending on Food Stamps (Not Controlling for Party Identification), 1988–1992

Explanatory variable	Coefficient	Standard error	T-statistic
Constant	1.51		
Age	.0002	.001	.11
Income	−.17	.02	7.26
Education	−.03	.02	2.14
Male	−.09	.04	2.13
African American	.44	.06	7.33
Southern	−.14	.05	2.81
Catholic	.02	.05	.41
Jewish	.20	.14	1.40
Suburban	−.14	.05	2.99
Homeowner	−.20	.05	3.99
Married with children	−.009	.05	.41

Source: American National Election Studies, 1988, 1990, and 1992 (Ann Arbor, Mich.: Inter-University Consortium for Political and Social Research, 1995).
Notes: Table entries are the results of ordered probit analysis. Positive numbers indicate pro-spending effects. N = 2,976. Log-likelihood = −2866.7. Threshold = 1.55.

Table 23. Warmth of Feeling toward Welfare Recipients, 1988–1992

Explanatory variable	Coefficient	Standard error	T-statistic
Constant	62.81		
Party identification	−1.10	.23	4.83
Age	.12	.03	4.10
Income	−1.58	.49	3.22
Education	−.36	.32	1.12
Male	−.25	.89	.28
African American	5.71	1.28	4.45
Southern	1.80	1.09	1.65
Catholic	.49	.99	.49
Jewish	−2.19	3.00	.73
Suburban	−2.18	.98	2.23
Homeowner	−2.68	1.04	2.56
Married with children	−.56	1.06	.53

Source: American National Election Studies, 1988, 1990, and 1992 (Ann Arbor, Mich.: Inter-University Consortium for Political and Social Research, 1995).
Notes: Table entries are the results of ordinary least squares analysis. Positive numbers indicate warmer feelings toward welfare recipients. $N = 3,060$.

Table 24. Support for Spending on Social Security, 1988–1992

Explanatory variable	Coefficient	Standard error	T-statistic
Constant	3.10		
Party identification	−.09	.01	7.79
Age	−.002	.001	1.40
Income	−.07	.03	2.88
Education	−.12	.02	7.11
Male	−.28	.05	6.18
African American	.36	.07	5.09
Southern	.15	.06	2.60
Catholic	.03	.05	.52
Jewish	−.19	.15	1.31
Suburban	−.002	.05	.04
Homeowner	−.02	.05	.30
Married with children	−.04	.05	.74

Source: American National Election Studies, 1988, 1990, and 1992 (Ann Arbor, Mich.: Inter-University Consortium for Political and Social Research, 1995).
Notes: Table entries are the results of ordered probit analysis. Positive numbers indicate pro-spending effects. $N = 3,021$. Log-likelihood $= -2239.7$. Threshold $= 1.70$.

Table 25. Correlation Coefficients for Suburban Characteristics, 1988–1992

Characteristics of suburban ring	Percentage black	Population decline
Percentage poor	.21	.13
Percentage black	—	.34

Sources: Bureau of the Census, *1990 Census of Population and Housing,* summary tape file 3C, 1992; *American National Election Studies, 1988, 1990, and 1992* (Ann Arbor, Mich.: Inter-University Consortium for Political and Social Research, 1995).
Note: Table entries are based on 1990 census data describing the suburban rings that were included in the National Election Studies sample of 1988–1992.

Table 26. Characteristics of Suburban Rings in the National Election Studies Sample, 1988–1992

Metropolitan area	Percentage population change, 1980–90	Percentage poor	Percentage black
Growing (+)			
Riverside–San Bernadino–Ontario, Calif.	73.2	11	6
Phoenix, Ariz.	58.3	12	2
Jacksonville, Fla.	49.7	9	8
Dallas–Ft. Worth, Tex.	48.2	7	6
Houston, Tex.	46.7	9	9
Atlanta, Ga.	43.4	7	19
McAllen–Pharr–Edinburg, Tex.	40.0	47	<1
Sacramento, Calif.	33.5	9	4
Seattle–Everett, Wash.	30.9	6	2
Richmond, Va.	30.0	6	18
Manchester, N.H.	25.7	3	<1
Anaheim–Santa Ana–Garden Grove, Calif.	24.7	7	2
Denver–Boulder, Colo.	23.7	7	3
Miami, Fla.	23.4	14	23
Waco, Tex.	23.1	11	6
Lakeland–Winter Haven, Fla.	22.5	12	11
Minneapolis–St. Paul, Minn.-Wisc.	22.1	5	1
Washington, D.C.-Md.-Va.	20.6	4	20
Des Moines, Iowa	20.0	5	1
Los Angeles–Long Beach, Calif.	19.3	12	9
Grand Rapids, Mich.	18.9	5	1
Baltimore, Md.	16.5	5	10
San Francisco–Oakland, Calif.	16.0	7	7
Atlantic City, N.J.	15.6	7	8

**Table 26 (*continued*). Characteristics of Suburban Rings in the National
Election Studies Sample, 1988–1992**

Metropolitan area	Percentage population change, 1980–90	Percentage poor	Percentage black
Worcester, Mass.	12.4	5	1
Knoxville, Tenn.	12.3	12	2
Kansas City, Mo.-Kans.	11.3	6	2
Dayton, Ohio	11.1	7	6
Philadelphia, Penn.-N.J.	8.0	5	8
New Haven–West Haven, Conn.	7.3	4	4
Birmingham, Ala.	7.1	10	9
St. Louis, Mo.-Ill.	6.5	7	10
Chicago, Ill.	6.1	4	7
Milwaukee, Wisc.	5.7	3	1
Fresno, Calif.	5.4	18	1
Fort Wayne, Ind.	4.9	4	1
Boston, Mass.	2.6	5	1
Detroit, Mich.	2.2	6	4
New York, N.Y.-N.J.	1.7	7	12
Nassau–Suffolk, N.Y.	0.1	4	7
Declining (−)			
Newark, N.J.	0.5	11	17
Buffalo, N.Y.	1.3	6	1
Eugene–Springfield, Oreg.	1.9	12	<1
Saginaw, Mich.	5.4	10	4
Pittsburgh, Penn.	6.1	10	4
Columbus, Ga.-Ala.	7.7	17	36
Steubenville–Weirton, Ohio-W.Va.	12.2	14	1
Wheeling, W.V.-Ohio	19.0	16	1

Sources: Bureau of the Census, *1990 Census of Population and Housing,* summary tape file
3C, 1992; *American National Election Studies, 1988, 1990, and 1992* (Ann Arbor, Mich.:
Inter-University Consortium for Political and Social Research, 1995).

Table 27. Relationship between Living in Certain Kinds of Suburbs and Vote Choice and Party Identification

Explanatory variable	Vote choice[a]		Party identification[b]
	President	Congress	
Constant	1.93	1.50	5.06
Age	−.009*	−.004	.004
	(.005)	(.005)	(.002)
Income	−.14	−.20*	−.15**
	(.08)	(.08)	(.04)
Education	−.15**	−.09	−.12**
	(.05)	(.05)	(.03)
Male	−.34**	−.22	−.18*
	(.13)	(.14)	(.07)
African American	1.89**	1.48**	1.24**
	(.24)	(.27)	(.10)
Southern	−.67**	−.29	−.05
	(.19)	(.19)	(.09)
Catholic	.16	.36*	.32**
	(.14)	(.15)	(.08)
Jewish	1.95**	1.20**	1.48**
	(.45)	(.44)	(.24)
Homeowner	−.01	.12	.13
	(.16)	(.17)	(.08)
Married with children	−.21	−.28	−.14
	(.16)	(.16)	(.08)
Democratic incumbent (Congress)	—	1.54**	—
		(.18)	
Republican incumbent (Congress)	—	−1.04**	—
		(.20)	
Suburb	−1.06**	−1.35**	−.81**
	(.21)	(.25)	(.11)
Declining suburb	.34	.02	.42**
	(.21)	(.25)	(.12)
Suburb, percentage poor	.02	−.03	.005
	(.02)	(.02)	(.008)
Suburb, percentage black	.06**	.11**	.03**
	(.01)	(.02)	(.006)
N	1,173	1,553	3,060
Log-likelihood	−703.87	−708.08	—

Sources: Bureau of the Census, *1990 Census of Population and Housing,* summary tape file 3C, 1992; *American National Election Studies, 1988, 1990, and 1992* (Ann Arbor, Mich.: Inter-University Consortium for Political and Social Research, 1995).

Notes: Positive numbers indicate pro-Democratic effects. Standard errors are shown in parentheses.

[a]Coefficients were derived from logit analysis.
[b]Coefficients were derived from ordinary least squares analysis.
*Significant at the .05 level.
**Significant at the .01 level.

Table 28. Relationship between Living in Certain Kinds of Suburbs and Support for Government Spending and Feelings toward Welfare Recipients

Explanatory variable	Food stamps[a]	Programs to assist blacks[a]	Feelings toward welfare recipients[b]
Constant	1.50	1.03	60.06
Age	.0003	.002	.12**
	(.001)	(.001)	(.03)
Income	−.17**	−.03	−1.76**
	(.02)	(.02)	(.50)
Education	−.03*	.02	−.45
	(.02)	(.02)	(.32)
Male	−.09*	−.11**	−.62
	(.04)	(.04)	(.89)
African American	.43**	1.08**	7.03**
	(.06)	(.07)	(1.27)
Southern	−.17	−.06	.32
	(.06)	(.06)	(1.20)
Catholic	.02	.06	.51
	(.05)	(.05)	(1.00)
Jewish	.20	.20	−.79
	(.14)	(.15)	(3.01)
Homeowner	−.20**	−.12*	−2.20*
	(.05)	(.05)	(1.06)
Married with children	−.01	−.02	−1.23
	(.05)	(.05)	(1.06)
Suburb	−.18**	−.32**	−4.47**
	(.07)	(.07)	(1.45)
Declining suburb	−.00009	−.23**	−4.55**
	(.07)	(.07)	(1.51)
Suburb, percentage poor	−.003	−.007	.02
	(.005)	(.005)	(.11)
Suburb, percentage black	.003	.02**	.24**
	(.004)	(.004)	(.08)
N	2,976	2,974	3,104
Log-likelihood	−2866.2	−2707.1	—
Threshold	1.55	1.67	—

Sources: Bureau of the Census, *1990 Census of Population and Housing,* summary tape file 3C, 1992; *American National Election Studies, 1988, 1990, and 1992* (Ann Arbor, Mich.: Inter-University Consortium for Political and Social Research, 1995).

Notes: Positive numbers indicate pro-spending and pro–welfare recipient effects. Standard errors are shown in parentheses.

[a]Coefficients were derived from ordered probit analysis.

[b]Coefficients were derived from ordinary least squares analysis.

*Significant at the .05 level.

**Significant at the .01 level.

Table 29. Relationship between Living in Certain Kinds of Suburbs and Support for Government Spending

Explanatory variable	Social Security[a]	General government spending and services[b]
Constant	2.82	6.12
Age	−.002	−.01**
	(.001)	(.002)
Income	−.08**	−.13**
	(.03)	(.03)
Education	−.13**	−.16**
	(.02)	(.02)
Male	−.31**	−.36**
	(.05)	(.06)
African American	.47**	.71**
	(.07)	(.09)
Southern	.19**	−.08
	(.06)	(.08)
Catholic	.05	.23**
	(.05)	(.07)
Jewish	−.04	.43*
	(.15)	(.20)
Homeowner	−.02	−.13
	(.05)	(.07)
Married with children	.03	−.12
	(.05)	(.07)
Suburb	.007	−.39**
	(.07)	(.10)
Declining suburb	.14	−.04
	(.08)	(.10)
Suburb, percentage poor	−.008	.006
	(.006)	(.007)
Suburb, percentage black	−.003	.01*
	(.004)	(.005)
N	3,057	2,616
Log-likelihood	−2219.9	—
Threshold	1.67	—

Sources: Bureau of the Census, *1990 Census of Population and Housing,* summary tape file 3C, 1992; *American National Election Studies, 1988, 1990, and 1992* (Ann Arbor, Mich.: Inter-University Consortium for Political and Social Research, 1995).

Notes: Positive numbers indicate pro-spending effects. Standard errors are shown in parentheses.

[a]Coefficients were derived from ordered probit analysis.

[b]Coefficients were derived from ordinary least squares analysis.

*Significant at the .05 level.

**Significant at the .01 level.

Table 30. Relationship between Type of Location and Probability of Supporting Republican Candidates and Expected Score on Party Identification

Location	Vote choice (% probability)		Expected party identification
	President	Congress	
City	44	46	3.9
Suburb: No population decline, no black population	70	77	3.1
Suburb: Population decline, no black population	—	—	3.5
Suburb: No population decline, 12% black population	53	47	3.4

Source: Table entries were derived from an interpretation of the coefficients in table 27.
Notes: All variables were held constant except location. Constants were as follows: thirty-five-year-old white Protestant woman, homeowner, married with children, mean education and income, 0 percent poverty rate.

Table 31. Relationship between Type of Location and Probability of Support for Spending to Assist Blacks and Expected Feelings toward Welfare Recipients

Location	Spending to assist blacks (% probability)		Expected feeling thermometer score
	Increase	Decrease	
City	36	25	53.7
Suburb: No population decline, no black population	29	32	49.2
Suburb: Population decline, no black population	24	37	44.7
Suburb: No population decline, 12% black population	34	27	52.1

Source: Table entries were derived from an interpretation of the coefficients in table 28.
Notes: All variables were held constant except location. Constants were as follows: fifty-year-old white Jewish man, homeowner, married with children, mean education and income, 0 percent poverty rate.

Table 32. Correlation Coefficients for Metropolitan Area Characteristics, 1988–1992

Characteristic of metropolitan area	No. of governments per million in population	Percentage poor (city − suburb)	Percentage black (city − suburb)	Population change	
				City	Suburb
Age	.39	.80	.75	−.20	.27
No. of governments (divided by population)	—	.33	.31	−.28	−.09
Percentage poor (city − suburb)	—	—	.84	−.34	.09
Percentage black (city − suburb)	—	—	—	−.31	.09

Sources: Bureau of the Census, *1990 Census of Population and Housing,* summary tape file 3C, 1992; *American National Election Studies, 1988, 1990, and 1992* (Ann Arbor, Mich.: Inter-University Consortium for Political and Social Research, 1995).

Table 33. Characteristics of Metropolitan Areas in the National Election Studies Sample, 1988–1992

Area and age[a]	No. of governments per million in population	Population change, city 1980–90	City-suburb difference	
			Percentage poor	Percentage black
1900 and earlier				
Atlanta, Ga.	29.1	−7.3	+18	+43
Baltimore, Md.	6.1	−6.5	+16	+48
Boston, Mass.	35.8	+2.0	+10	+12
Buffalo, N.Y.	63.0	−8.3	+18	+27
Chicago, Ill.	22.2	−7.4	+18	+32
Dayton, Ohio	86.7	−5.9	+9	+28
Denver–Boulder, Colo.	20.5	−.5	+9	+7
Detroit, Mich.	49.8	−14.6	+26	+72
Grand Rapids, Mich.	82.9	+4.0	+10	+15
Kansas City, Mo.-Kans.	64.4	−7.1	+12	+24
Los Angeles– Long Beach, Calif.	9.4	+17.6	+6	+45
Manchester, N.H.	5.0	+9.5	+6	+1
Milwaukee, Wisc.	64.3	−1.3	+17	+26
Minneapolis–St. Paul., Minn.	115.0	−.1	+11	+8
Nassau–Suffolk, N.Y.	41.9	+3.5	+15	+45
Newark, N.J.	64.4	−16.4	+15	+42
New Haven–West Haven, Conn.	35.0	+2.9	+17	+32
New York, N.Y.-N.J.	9.2	+3.5	+12	+40

Table 33 (*continued*). **Characteristics of Metropolitan Areas in the National Election Studies Sample, 1988–1992**

Area and age[a]	No. of governments per million in population	Population change, city 1980–90	City-suburb difference Percentage poor	City-suburb difference Percentage black
Philadelphia, Penn.-N.J.	69.2	−6.1	+15	+32
Pittsburgh, Penn.	149.0	−12.8	+12	+22
Richmond, Va.	3.3	−7.4	+15	+37
San Francisco– Oakland, Calif.	17.3	+7.6	+10	+15
Seattle–Everett, Wash.	23.5	+6.9	+6	+8
St. Louis, Mo.-Ill.	83.8	−12.4	+15	+30
Washington, D.C.-Md.-Va.	17.8	−4.9	+10	+31
Worcester, Mass.	62.5	+4.9	+9	+3
1910				
Birmingham, Ala.	52.0	−6.5	+15	+54
Dallas–Ft. Worth, Tex.	45.9	+12.8	+9	+16
Des Moines, Iowa	75.0	+1.1	+7	+6
Houston, Tex.	30.6	+2.2	+12	+19
1920				
Fort Wayne, Ind.	57.5	+.4	+7	+16
Jacksonville, Fla.	18.9	+17.4	+4	+17
Knoxville, Tenn.	43.3	−5.7	+6	+13
Saginaw, Mich.	175.0	−10.3	+22	+36
Wheeling, W.Va.-Ohio	120.0	−19.0	0	+3
1930				
Atlantic City, N.J.	8.8	−5.5	+17	+42
Fresno, Calif.	21.4	+62.9	+5	+7
Miami, Fla.	13.7	+3.4	+17	+4
Sacramento, Calif.	9.3	+34.0	+7	+5
1940				
Columbus, Ga.-Ala.	25.0	+5.3	+1	+2
Phoenix, Ariz.	10.0	+24.5	0	+2
Waco, Tex.	100.0	+2.3	+16	+17
1950				
Anaheim–Santa Ana– Garden Grove, Calif.	8.7	+32.3	+8	+1
Riverside–San Bernadino– Ontario, Calif.	14.2	+35.0	+6	+5
1960				
Eugene–Springfield, Oreg.	40.0	+6.8	+4	+1
1970 and later				
Lakeland–Winter Haven, Fla.	42.5	+39.1	+1	+10
McAllen–Pharr– Edinburg, Tex.	45.0	+31.4	−12	0
Steubenville– Weirton, Ohio-W.Va.	270.0	−14.5	+2	+9

Sources: Bureau of the Census, *1990 Census of Population and Housing,* Summary tape file 3C, 1992; *American National Election Studies, 1988, 1990, and 1992* (Ann Arbor, Mich.: Inter-University Consortium for Political and Social Research, 1995).

[a]Groupings by age were determined by the year in which the center-city population reached 50,000.

Table 34. Relationship between Living in a Particular Metropolitan Area and Vote Choice and Party Identification

Where respondent lives	Vote choice[a]		Party identification[b]
	President	Congress	
Model 1: Age			
Metropolitan area	.05	−.04	.05**
	(.04)	(.04)	(.02)
Suburban ring (suburb × metro)	−.09**	−.11**	−.08**
	(.02)	(.03)	(.01)
Model 2: Number of governments			
Metropolitan area	.006**	.005	.006**
	(.002)	(.003)	(.001)
Suburban ring (suburb × metro)	−.006**	−.006*	−.004**
	(.002)	(.002)	(.001)
Model 3: City-suburb difference in poverty rate			
Metropolitan area	−.002	.007	.01
	(.01)	(.02)	(.007)
Suburban ring (suburb × metro)	−.05**	−.06**	−.04**
	(.01)	(.01)	(.007)
Model 4: City-suburb difference in the proportion of the population that is black			
Metropolitan area	.01	.01	.01**
	(.006)	(.007)	(.003)
Suburban ring (suburb × metro)	−.02**	−.02**	−.02**
	(.006)	(.007)	(.003)
Model 5: Population change			
Metropolitan area—City	−.02*	−.007	−.006*
	(.008)	(.007)	(.004)
Suburban ring (suburb × metro)	.02*	.03**	.009*
	(.009)	(.009)	(.005)
Metropolitan area—Suburb	.006	.01*	−.002
	(.005)	(.006)	(.003)
Suburban ring (suburb × metro)	−.01	−.03**	−.01**
	(.007)	(.007)	(.004)

Sources: Bureau of the Census, *1990 Census of Population and Housing,* summary tape file 3C, 1992; *American National Election Studies, 1988, 1990, and 1992* (Ann Arbor, Mich.: Inter-University Consortium for Political and Social Research, 1995).

Notes: Table entries show the results of running five separate models for each dependent variable. Each of the five included the two location variables as shown in the table, in addition to controls for age, education, income, gender, race, living in the South, religion, homeownership, being married with children, and incumbency (congressional vote choice only). The suburban ring variable was formed by multiplying a dummy variable for living in a suburb by the variable describing the metropolitan area. Positive numbers indicate pro-Democratic effects. Standard errors are shown in parentheses.

[a]Coefficients were derived from logit analysis.

[b]Coefficients were derived from ordinary least squares analysis.

*Significant at the .05 level.

**Significant at the .01 level.

Table 35. Relationship between Living in a Particular Metropolitan Area and Support for Government Spending and Feelings toward Welfare Recipients

Where respondent lives	Support for spending on		Feelings towards welfare recipients[b]
	Food stamps[a]	Programs to assist blacks[a]	
Model 1: Age			
Metropolitan area	.07**	.02*	.19
	(.01)	(.01)	(.25)
Suburban ring (suburb × metro)	−.02**	−.04**	−.45**
	(.008)	(.008)	(.17)
Model 2: Number of governments			
Metropolitan area	.000005	.0007	.02
	(.0007)	(.0007)	(.01)
Suburban ring (suburb × metro)	−.001	−.002**	−.04**
	(.0007)	(.0007)	(.01)
Model 3: City-suburb difference in poverty rate			
Metropolitan area	.02**	.003	.11
	(.004)	(.005)	(.09)
Suburban ring (suburb × metro)	−.02**	−.02**	−.26**
	(.004)	(.004)	(.09)
Model 4: City-suburb difference in the proportion of the population that is black			
Metropolitan area	.008**	.004**	.04
	(.002)	(.002)	(.04)
Suburban ring (suburb × metro)	−.007**	−.009**	−.10*
	(.002)	(.002)	(.04)
Model 5: Population change			
Metropolitan area—City	−.0009	−.0005	−.09*
	(.002)	(.002)	(.05)
Suburban ring (suburb × metro)	−.0002	.005	.09
	(.003)	(.003)	(.06)
Metropolitan area—Suburb	−.002	.003	.09*
	(.002)	(.002)	(.04)
Suburban ring (suburb × metro)	−.003	−.003	−.007
	(.002)	(.002)	(.05)

Sources: Bureau of the Census, *1990 Census of Population and Housing,* summary tape file 3C, 1992; *American National Election Studies, 1988, 1990, and 1992* (Ann Arbor, Mich.: Inter-University Consortium for Political and Social Research, 1995).
Notes: Table entries show the results of running five separate models for each dependent variable. Each of the five included the two location variables as shown in the table, in addition to controls for age, education, income, gender, race, living in the South, religion, homeownership, being married with children, and incumbency (congressional vote choice only). The suburban ring variable was formed by multiplying a dummy variable for living in a suburb by the variable describing the metropolitan area. Positive numbers indicate pro-spending and pro–welfare recipient effects. Standard errors are shown in parentheses.
[a]Coefficients were derived from ordered probit analysis.
[b]Coefficients were derived from ordinary least squares analysis.
*Significant at the .05 level.
**Significant at the .01 level.

Table 36. Relationship between Living in a Particular Metropolitan Area and Support for Government Spending

Where respondent lives	Support for spending on Social Security[a]	Support for general government spending and services[b]
Model 1: Age		
Metropolitan area	.02	.03
	(.01)	(.02)
Suburban ring (suburb × metro)	−.01	−.04**
	(.009)	(.01)
Model 2: Number of governments		
Metropolitan area	.0007	.001
	(.0007)	(.001)
Suburban ring (suburb × metro)	−.0003	−.003**
	(.0007)	(.001)
Model 3: City-suburb difference in poverty rate		
Metropolitan area	.006	.007
	(.005)	(.006)
Suburban ring (suburb × metro)	−.006	−.02**
	(.004)	(.006)
Model 4: City-suburb difference in the proportion of the population that is black		
Metropolitan area	.006**	.005
	(.002)	(.003)
Suburban ring (suburb × metro)	−.006**	−.008**
	(.002)	(.003)
Model 5: Population change		
Metropolitan area—City	.001	.008*
	(.002)	(.003)
Suburban ring (suburb × metro)	.0006	−.007
	(.003)	(.004)
Metropolitan area—Suburb	−.003	−.003
	(.002)	(.002)
Suburban ring (suburb × metro)	−.003	−.001
	(.002)	(.003)

Sources: Bureau of the Census, *1990 Census of Population and Housing,* summary tape file 3C, 1992; *American National Election Studies, 1988, 1990, and 1992* (Ann Arbor, Mich.: Inter-University Consortium for Political and Social Research, 1995).

Notes: Table entries show the results of running five separate models for each dependent variable. Each of the five included the two location variables as shown in the table, in addition to controls for age, education, income, gender, race, living in the South, religion, homeownership, being married with children, and incumbency (congressional vote choice only). The suburban ring variable was formed by multiplying a dummy variable for living in a suburb by the variable describing the metropolitan area. Positive numbers indicate pro-spending effects. Standard errors are shown in parentheses.

[a]Coefficients were derived from ordered probit analysis.

[b]Coefficients were derived from ordinary least squares analysis.

*Significant at the .05 level.

**Significant at the .01 level.

Table 37. Probability of Supporting Republican Candidates and Expected Party Identification

| Location | Vote choice (% probability) | | Expected party identification score |
	President	Congress	
6% difference in poverty rates			
City	43	40	4.5
Suburb	50	48	4.2
Difference	7	8	.3
18% difference in poverty rates			
City	43	38	4.6
Suburb	65	64	3.9
Difference	22	26	.7

Source: Table entries are interpretations of coefficients in table 34.
Notes: All variables were held constant except location. Constants were as follows: fifty-year-old white Catholic woman, some college, not living in the South, homeowner, married with children, income in the 34th–67th percentile.

Table 38. Probability of Supporting Spending to Assist Blacks and Expected Score on Feeling Thermometer

| Location | Spending to assist blacks | | Expected score on feeling thermometer |
	Decrease	Increase	
6% difference in poverty rates			
City	36	25	55.3
Suburb	33	28	53.8
Difference	3	3	1.5
18% difference in poverty rates			
City	37	25	56.6
Suburb	29	32	52.0
Difference	8	7	4.6

Source: Table entries are interpretations of coefficients in table 35.
Notes: All variables were held constant except location. Constants were as follows: fifty-year-old white Catholic woman, some college, not living in the South, homeowner, married with children, income in the 34th–67th percentile.

Table 39. Number of Congressional Districts by Type, 1973–1993

District type	60% scheme 1973	60% scheme 1985	60% scheme 1993	50% scheme 1973	50% scheme 1985	50% scheme 1993
Urban	78	73	67	102	98	82
Change		−5	−6		−4	−16
Suburban	88	129	160	131	170	212
Change		+41	+31		+39	+42
Rural	92	61	57	130	88	77
Change		−31	−4		−42	−11
Mixed	177	172	151	72	79	64
Change		−5	−21		−7	−15
Total	435					

Source: Data collected by David Huckabee for the Congressional Research Service.

Table 40. Correlation between Various Characteristics of Congressional Districts, 101st–103rd Congress

Characteristics	Percentage suburban
Percentage African American	−.34
Percentage with high school education or above	.39
Median family income	.36

Source: The suburban variable was supplied by David Huckabee of the Congressional Research Service. The other variables were drawn from David Lublin's congressional data set, which includes data from *1980 Census of Population and Housing; Congressional Districts of the 98th Congress* (Washington, D.C.: GPO, 1983); *1980 Census of Population and Housing: Congressional Districts of the 99th Congress* (Washington, D.C.: GPO, 1984); *1980 Census of Population and Housing: Congressional Districts of the 100th Congress, Ohio* (Washington, D.C.: GPO, 1986); and *1990 Census of Population and Housing: Population and Housing Characteristics of the 103rd Congress* (Washington, D.C.: GPO, 1992).
Note: Data analysis by author.

Table 41. Party of Congressional Representative by Type of District, 101st–103rd Congress

District type	Democrats (%)	Republicans (%)
Suburban	51	49
Urban	84	16

Source: The suburban variable was supplied by David Huckabee of the Congressional Research Service. The other variables were drawn from David Lublin's congressional data set, which includes data from *1980 Census of Population and Housing; Congressional Districts of the 98th Congress* (Washington, D.C.: GPO, 1983); *1980 Census of Population and Housing: Congressional Districts of the 99th Congress* (Washington, D.C.: GPO, 1984); *1980 Census of Population and Housing: Congressional Districts of the 100th Congress, Ohio* (Washington, D.C.: GPO, 1986); and *1990 Census of Population and Housing: Population and Housing Characteristics of the 103rd Congress* (Washington, D.C.: GPO, 1992).

Note: Data analysis by author. Suburban = more than 50 percent suburban residents. Urban = more than 50 percent city residents.

Table 42. Party of Congressional Representative, 101st–103rd Congress

Explanatory variable	Coefficient	Standard error	T-statistic
Constant	6.92		
Length of service	.03	.02	1.34
Republican incumbent	−6.31	.33	19.34
Open seat	−2.58	.35	7.47
Percentage of constituents over 65 years old	.01	.04	.30
Median family income	.000006	.00002	.13
Percentage with high school education or above	−.05	.02	2.45
Percentage black	.05	.02	3.08
Southern	−.74	.35	2.14
Percentage suburban	−.01	.006	1.99
Percentage rural	−.01	.006	2.19

Source: The suburban variable was supplied by David Huckabee of the Congressional Research Service. The other variables were drawn from David Lublin's congressional data set, which includes data from *1980 Census of Population and Housing; Congressional Districts of the 98th Congress* (Washington, D.C.: GPO, 1983); *1980 Census of Population and Housing: Congressional Districts of the 99th Congress* (Washington, D.C.: GPO, 1984); *1980 Census of Population and Housing: Congressional Districts of the 100th Congress, Ohio* (Washington, D.C.: GPO, 1986); and *1990 Census of Population and Housing: Population and Housing Characteristics of the 103rd Congress* (Washington, D.C.: GPO, 1992).

Notes: Table entries are the results of logit analysis. Positive numbers indicate pro-Democratic effects. $N = 1,299$. Log-likelihood = -249.48.

Table 43. Probability That a Congressional District Is Represented by a Republican

District type	Probability (%)
10% suburban 90% urban	17
50% suburban 50% urban	24
90% suburban 10% urban	31

Source: Table entries were derived from an interpretation of the coefficient in table 42.

Notes: All variables were held constant except location. Constants were as follows: non-Southern district with no incumbent, 5 percent African American population, all other variables held constant at their mean.

Table 44. Democratic Proportion of the Vote for Members of the 101st–103rd Congresses

Explanatory variable	Coefficient	Standard error	T-statistic
Constant	92.23		
Length of service	.005	.05	.10
Republican incumbent	−36.92	.93	39.87
Open seat	−14.18	1.46	9.69
Percentage of constituents over 　sixty-five years old	.008	.13	.06
Median family income	−.000004	.00009	.07
Percentage with high school 　education or above	−.25	.06	4.17
Percentage black	.19	.03	5.82
Southern	−3.11	1.07	2.92
Percentage suburban	−.09	.02	5.07
Percentage rural	−.09	.02	4.91

Source: The suburban variable was supplied by David Huckabee of the Congressional Research Service. The other variables were drawn from David Lublin's congressional data set, which includes data from *1980 Census of Population and Housing; Congressional Districts of the 98th Congress* (Washington, D.C.: GPO, 1983); *1980 Census of Population and Housing: Congressional Districts of the 99th Congress* (Washington, D.C.: GPO, 1984); *1980 Census of Population and Housing: Congressional Districts of the 100th Congress, Ohio* (Washington, D.C.: GPO, 1986); and *1990 Census of Population and Housing: Population and Housing Characteristics of the 103rd Congress* (Washington, D.C.: GPO, 1992).

Notes: Table entries are the results of ordinary least squares analysis. Positive numbers indicate pro-Democratic effects. $N = 1,286$.

Table 45. Mean Poole-Rosenthal Scores by Party and District Type,
101st–103rd Congresses

District type	Party	Mean score[a]	Difference
More than 50% suburban	Democrat	−.299	
More than 50% urban	Democrat	−.384	.085
More than 50% suburban	Republican	.329	
More than 50% urban	Republican	.311	.018
More than 70% suburban	Democrat	−.310	
More than 70% urban	Democrat	−.417	.107
More than 70% suburban	Republican	.328	
More than 70% urban	Republican	.257	.071

Source: Poole-Rosenthal Web site, <http://K7moa.gsia.cmu.edu>.
Note: The higher the score, the more conservative the member's ideology.

Table 46. Poole-Rosenthal Scores of Congressional Representatives,
101st–103rd Congresses

Explanatory variable	Coefficient	Standard error	T-statistic
Constant	.38		
Length of service	−.002	.0005	3.88
Percentage of constituents over sixty-five years old	.005	.001	4.21
Democrat	−.60	.01	46.14
Democratic proportion of vote	.07	.03	2.44
Median family income	.0000005	.0000006	
Percentage with high school education or above	−.0009	.0006	1.47
Percentage black	−.003	.0003	10.53
Southern	.12	.01	11.51
Percentage suburban	.0004	.0002	2.26
Percentage rural	.001	.0002	5.86

Sources: David Lublin's congressional data set, which includes data from *1980 Census of Population and Housing; Congressional Districts of the 98th Congress* (Washington, D.C.: GPO, 1983); *1980 Census of Population and Housing: Congressional Districts of the 99th Congress* (Washington, D.C.: GPO, 1984); *1980 Census of Population and Housing: Congressional Districts of the 100th Congress, Ohio* (Washington, D.C.: GPO, 1986); and *1990 Census of Population and Housing: Population and Housing Characteristics of the 103rd Congress* (Washington, D.C.: GPO, 1992); Poole-Rosenthal Web site, <http://K7moa.gsia.cmu.edu>.
Notes: Table entries are the results of ordinary least squares analysis. Positive numbers indicate movement in a more liberal direction. $N = 1,290$.

**Table 47. League of Cities Scores for Congressional Representatives,
101st–103rd Congresses**

Explanatory variable	Coefficient	Standard error	T-statistic
Constant	49.26		
Length of service	.03	.07	.38
Percentage of constituents over sixty-five years old	.24	.19	1.26
Median income	−.0003	.00009	3.09
Democratic proportion of vote	9.18	4.27	2.15
Percentage with high school education or above	−.12	.09	1.27
Percentage black	−.07	.05	1.42
Southern	−7.03	1.59	4.41
Percentage suburban	.01	.03	.38
Percentage rural	−.15	.03	5.07
Democrat	29.28	2.02	14.48

Sources: David Lublin's congressional data set, which includes data from *1980 Census of Population and Housing; Congressional Districts of the 98th Congress* (Washington, D.C.: GPO, 1983); *1980 Census of Population and Housing: Congressional Districts of the 99th Congress* (Washington, D.C.: GPO, 1984); *1980 Census of Population and Housing: Congressional Districts of the 100th Congress, Ohio* (Washington, D.C.: GPO, 1986); and *1990 Census of Population and Housing: Population and Housing Characteristics of the 103rd Congress* (Washington, D.C.: GPO, 1992); data provided by the Center for Policy and Federal Relations, National League of Cities.
Notes: Table entries are the results of ordinary least squares analysis. Positive numbers indicate increasing support for the League of Cities' agenda. $N = 1,270$.

Bibliography

Abbott, Carl. *The New Urban America: Growth and Politics in Sunbelt Cities.* Chapel Hill: University of North Carolina Press, 1987.

"A Houston Suburb That Said No to a Democrat, after Forty-Two Years." *New York Times,* 19 December 1994, sec. B.

American National Election Studies, 1948–1994. Ann Arbor, Mich.: Inter-University Consortium for Political and Social Research, 1995.

Ayres, B. Drummond Jr. "Los Angeles, Long Fragmented, Faces Threat of Secession by the San Fernando Valley." *New York Times,* 29 May 1996, sec. A.

Baldassare, Mark. *Trouble in Paradise: The Suburban Transformation in America.* New York: Columbia University Press, 1986.

Bell, Michael E., ed. *Research in Urban Economics: State and Local Finance in an Era of New Federalism.* Greenwich, Conn.: JAI Press, 1988.

Berger, Bennet M. *Working-Class Suburb.* Berkeley and Los Angeles: University of California Press, 1960.

Blakely, Edward J., and Mary Gail Snyder. *Fortress America: Gated Communities in the United States.* Washington, D.C.: Brookings

Institution Press; Cambridge, Mass.: Lincoln Institute of Land Policy, 1997.

Bledsoe, Timothy, and Susan Welch. "Residential Context and Racial Solidarity among African Americans." *American Journal of Political Science* 39, no. 2 (May 1995).

Bogue, Donald J. *Population Growth in Standard Metropolitan Areas 1900–1950.* Washington, D.C.: GPO, 1953.

Books, John W., and Charles L. Prysby. *Political Behavior and the Local Context.* New York: Praeger, 1991.

Boyle, T. Coraghessan. *The Tortilla Curtain.* New York: Penguin Books, 1995.

Bradbury, Katherine L., Anthony Downs, and Kenneth A. Small. *Urban Decline and the Future of American Cities.* Washington, D.C.: Brookings Institution Press, 1982.

Briffault, Richard. "Localism and Legal Theory (Our Localism, Part 2)." *Columbia Law Review* 90, no. 2 (March 1990).

Brown, Thad A. *Migration and Politics: The Impact of Population Mobility on American Voting Behavior.* Chapel Hill: University of North Carolina Press, 1988.

Buchanan, James M. "Principles of Urban Fiscal Strategy." *Public Choice* 4 (fall 1971).

Burns, Nancy. *The Formation of American Local Governments: Private Values in Public Institutions.* New York: Oxford University Press, 1994.

Butler, David, and Donald Stokes. *Political Change in Britain.* New York: St. Martin's Press, 1969.

California Assembly Office of Research. *Getting Ahead of the Growth Curve: The Future of Local Government in California.* Sacramento, December 1989.

Caraley, Demetrios. "Carter, Congress, and the Cities." In *Urban Policy Making,* edited by Dale Rogers Marshall. Beverly Hills: Sage Publications, 1979.

———. "Washington Abandons the Cities." *Political Science Quarterly* 107, no. 1 (spring 1992).

Caraley, Demetrios, and Yvette R. Schlussel. "Congress and Reagan's New Federalism." *Publius: The Journal of Federalism* 16, no. 1 (winter 1986).

Cleaveland, Frederic N. *Congress and Urban Problems: A Casebook of the Legislative Process.* Washington, D.C.: Brookings Institution Press, 1969.

Congressional Quarterly Almanac 1980. Washington, D.C.: CQ Press, 1980.

Congressional Quarterly Almanac 1984. Washington, D.C.: CQ Press, 1984.

Congressional Quarterly Almanac 1992. Washington, D.C.: CQ Press, 1992.

Congressional Quarterly Weekly Report, 17 August 1996.

Congressional Quarterly Weekly Report, Democratic Convention Supplement, 17 August 1996.

Congressional Record. 94th Cong., 1st sess., 1975. Vol. 121, pt. 24.

Conlan, Timothy. *New Federalism: Intergovernmental Reform from Nixon to Reagan.* Washington, D.C.: Brookings Institution Press, 1988.

Cook, Rhodes. "As Suburban Loyalty Is Tested, Bush Isn't Making the Grade." *Congressional Quarterly Weekly Report,* 26 September 1992.

Cutler, David, and Jacob Vigdor. "The Rise of a Suburban Ghetto? Trends and Costs for African-American Families." Paper presented at the Suburban Racial Change Conference, Harvard University, Cambridge, Mass., 28 March 1998.

Danielson, Michael D. *The Politics of Exclusion.* New York: Columbia University Press, 1976.

Davis, Mike. *City of Quartz: Excavating the Future in Los Angeles.* New York: Vintage Books, 1990.

Denton, Nancy A., and Richard Alba. "Suburban Racial and Ethnic Change at the Neighborhood Level: The Declining Number of All-White Neighborhoods." Paper presented at the Suburban Racial Change Conference, Harvard University, Cambridge, Mass., 28 March 1998.

DeParle, Jason. "U.S. Welfare System Dies As State Programs Emerge." *New York Times,* 30 June 1997, sec. A.

De Witt, Karen. "Suburbs, Especially in the South, Are Becoming the Source of Political Power in the U.S." *New York Times,* 19 December 1994, sec. B.

Dionne, E. J., Jr. *Why Americans Hate Politics.* New York: Simon and Schuster, 1991.

Donovan, Todd, and Max Neiman. "Citizen Mobilization and the Adoption of Local Growth Control." *Western Political Quarterly* 45, no. 3 (September 1992).

———. "Community Social Status, Suburban Growth, and Local Government Restrictions on Residential Development." *Urban Affairs Quarterly* 28, no. 2 (December 1992).

Downs, Anthony. *New Visions for Metropolitan America.* Washington, D.C.: Brookings Institution Press; Cambridge, Mass.: Lincoln Institute of Land Policy, 1994.

Dreier, Peter. "Putting Cities on the National Agenda." *Urban Affairs Review* 30, no. 5 (May 1995).

———. "America's Urban Crisis: Symptoms, Causes, and Solutions." In *Race, Poverty, and American Cities,* edited by John Charles Boger and Judith Welch Wegner. Chapel Hill: University of North Carolina Press, 1996.

Drew, Elizabeth. *Showdown: The Struggle between the Gingrich Congress and the Clinton White House.* New York: Simon and Schuster, 1996.

Duff, Christina. "Plans for Census 'Sampling' Anger GOP in Congress." *Wall Street Journal,* 12 June 1997, sec. A.

Dye, Thomas. *American Federalism: Competition among Governments.* Lexington, Mass.: D.C. Heath, 1990.

Edsall, Thomas Byrne, and Mary D. Edsall. *Chain Reaction: The Impact of Race, Rights, and Taxes on American Politics.* New York: W.W. Norton, 1992.

Fishman, Robert. *Bourgeois Utopias: The Rise and Fall of Suburbia.* New York: Basic Books, 1987.

———. "America's New City: Megalopolis Unbound." *Wilson Quarterly* (winter 1990).

Fleischmann, Arnold, and Carol A. Pierannunzi. "Citizens, Development Interests, and Local Land-Use Regulation." *Journal of Politics* 52, no. 3 (August 1990).

Frey, William H. "Immigration, Domestic Migration, and Demographic Balkanization in America: New Evidence for the 1990s." *Population and Development Review* 22, no. 4 (December 1996).

Frey, William H., and Douglas Geverdt. "Changing Suburban Demographics: Beyond the 'Black-White, City-Suburb' Typology." Paper presented at the Suburban Racial Change Conference, Harvard University, Cambridge, Mass., 28 March 1998.

Frey, William H., and Alden Speare Jr. *Regional and Metropolitan Growth and Decline in the United States.* New York: Russell Sage Foundation, 1988.

Frug, Gerald E. "Decentering Decentralization." *University of Chicago Law Review* 60, no. 2 (spring 1993).

———. *Citymaking: Building Communities without Building Walls.* Princeton: Princeton University Press, 1999.

Gans, Herbert J. *The Levittowners.* New York: Pantheon Books, 1967.

Garland, Susan B. "The Battle of the 'Burbs: Redrawing the Political Map." *Business Week*, 26 November 1990.

Garreau, Joel. *Edge City: Life on the New Frontier.* New York: Doubleday, 1991.

Glaberson, William. "For Many in the New York Region, the City Is Ignored and Irrelevant." *New York Times,* 2 January 1992, sec. A.

Glaser, James M. "Back to the Black Belt: Racial Environment and White Racial Attitudes in the South." *Journal of Politics* 56, no. 1 (February 1994).

Goldberg, Carez. "Political Battle of the Sexes Is Tougher than Ever; Suburbs' Soccer Moms, Fleeing the G.O.P., Are Much Sought." *New York Times,* 6 October 1996, sec. A.

Greenberg, Stanley B. *Middle Class Dreams: The Politics and Power of the New American Majority.* New York: Times Books, 1995.

Greer, Ann Lennarson, and Scott Greer. "Suburban Political Behavior: A Matter of Trust." In *The Changing Face of the Suburbs,* edited by Barry Schwartz. Chicago: University of Chicago Press, 1976.

Halpern, Robert. *Rebuilding the Inner City: A History of Neighborhood Initiatives to Address Poverty in the United States.* New York: Columbia University Press, 1995.

Hill, Edward W., Harold L. Wolman, and Coit Cook Ford III. "Can Suburbs Survive without Their Central Cities? Examining the Suburban Dependence Hypothesis." *Urban Affairs Review* 31, no. 2 (November 1995).

Hirsch, Herbert. "Suburban Voting and National Trends: A Research Note." *Western Political Quarterly* 21, no. 3 (September 1968).

Huckabee, David C. "Congressional Districts of the 99th Congress Classified on an Urban to Rural Continuum." Report prepared for the Congressional Research Service. Washington, D.C.: Congressional Research Service, 9 September 1985.

Huckfeldt, Robert. "Ethnic Politics." *American Politics Quarterly* 11, no. 1 (January 1983).

Huckfeldt, Robert, and John Sprague. "Networks in Context: The Social Flow of Political Information." *American Political Science Review* 81, no. 4 (December 1987).

———. "Citizens, Contexts, and Politics." In *Political Science: The State of the Discipline II,* edited by Ada W. Finifter. Washington, D.C.: American Political Science Association, 1993.

Jackson, Kenneth T. *Crabgrass Frontier: The Suburbanization of the United States.* Oxford: Oxford University Press, 1985.

Jencks, Christopher, and Susan E. Mayer. "The Social Consequences of Growing Up in a Poor Neighborhood." In *Inner-City Poverty in the United States,* edited by Laurence E. Lynn Jr. and Michael G. H. McGeary. Washington, D.C.: National Academy Press, 1990.

Johnson, Donald Bruce, ed., *National Party Platforms, Volume II, 1960–1976.* (Urbana: University of Illinois Press, 1978).

Kasarda, John D. "Cities as Places Where People Live and Work: Urban Change and Neighborhood Distress." In *Urban Change in the United States and Western Europe: Comparative Analysis and Policy,* edited by Anita A. Summers, Paul C. Cheshire, and Lanfrenco Senn. Washington, D.C.: Urban Institute Press, 1993.

Kinder, Donald R., and Tali Mendelberg. "Cracks in American Apartheid: The Political Impact of Prejudice among Desegregated Whites." *Journal of Politics* 57, no. 2 (May 1995).

Kolata, Gina. "Vying for the Breast Vote." *New York Times,* 6 November 1996, sec. D.

Kolbert, Elizabeth. "Region around New York Sees Ties to City Faltering." *New York Times,* 1 December 1991, sec. A.

Kramer, John. *North American Suburbs: Politics, Diversity, and Change.* Berkeley: Glendessary Press, 1972.

Kranish, Michael, and Brian McGrory. "Suburbs Are Key in Clinton Election Plan." *Boston Globe,* 1 September 1996, sec. A.

Langdon, Philip. *A Better Place to Live: Reshaping the American Suburb.* Amherst: University of Massachusetts Press, 1994.

Lehne, Richard. "Shape of the Future." *National Civic Review* 58 (September 1969).

Liner, E. Blaine, ed. *A Decade of Devolution: Perspectives on State-Local Relations.* Washington, D.C.: Urban Institute Press, 1989.

Loth, Renee. "Citifying Suburbia: It Isn't What It Was, US Census Figures Show." *Boston Globe,* 3 November 1991, sec. B.

Lublin, David. *The Paradox of Representation: Racial Gerrymandering and Minority Interests in Congress.* Princeton: Princeton University Press, 1997.

Luppo, Alan. "'So What?' Says Suburbia." *Boston Globe,* 10 September 1993, sec. C.

MacKuen, Michael, and Courtney Brown. "Political Context and Attitude Change." *American Political Science Review* 81, no. 2 (June 1987).

Masotti, Louis H. "Prologue: Suburbia Reconsidered—Myth and Counter-Myth." In *The Urbanization of the Suburbs,* edited by Louis H. Masotti and Jeffrey K. Hadden. Beverly Hills: Sage Publications, 1973.

Masotti, Louis H., and Jeffrey K. Hadden, eds. *The Urbanization of the Suburbs.* Beverly Hills: Sage Publications, 1973.

Massey, Douglas S., and Nancy A. Denton. *American Apartheid: Segregation and the Making of the Underclass.* Cambridge, Mass.: Harvard University Press, 1993.

Massey, Douglas S., and Andrew B. Gross. "Explaining Trends in Residential Segregation, 1970–1980." *Urban Affairs Quarterly* 27, no. 1 (September 1991).

McKenzie, Evan. *Privatopia: Homeowner Associations and the Rise of Residential Private Government.* New Haven: Yale University Press, 1994.

Mead, Lawrence M. *Beyond Entitlement: The Social Obligations of Citizenship.* New York: Free Press, 1986.

Mergendahl, Charles. *It's Only Temporary.* New York: Doubleday, 1950.

Merry, Robert W. "Suburbia Ascendant: Dawn of a New Era." *Congressional Quarterly Weekly Report,* 29 June 1992.

Miller, Gary. *Cities by Contract: The Politics of Municipal Incorporation.* Cambridge, Mass.: MIT Press, 1981.

Mitchell, Alison. "Clinton Campaign Puts an Emphasis on Female Voters." *New York Times,* 28 October 1996, A1.

Morris, Dick. *Behind the Oval Office: Winning the Presidency in the 1990s.* New York: Random House, 1997.

Muller, Peter O. *Contemporary Suburban America.* Englewood Cliffs, N.J.: Prentice-Hall, 1981.

Murphy, Thomas P. *The New Politics of Congress.* Lexington, Mass.: Lexington Books, 1974.

Murray, Charles. *Losing Ground: American Social Policy, 1950–1980.* New York: Basic Books, 1984.

Newman, Katherine S. *Declining Fortunes: The Withering of the American Dream.* New York: Basic Books, 1993.

Oliver, J. Eric. "The Effects of Metropolitan Economic Segregation on Local Civic Participation." *American Journal of Political Science* 43, no. 1 (January 1999).

Orfield, Myron. *Metropolitics: A Regional Agenda for Community and Stability.* Washington, D.C.: Brookings Institution Press; Cambridge, Mass.: Lincoln Institute of Land Policy, 1997.

Pareles, Jon. "Newt Age Music." *New York Times,* 15 January 1995, sec. B.

Parker, Andrew R. "Patterns of Federal Urban Spending: Central Cities and Their Suburbs, 1983–1992." *Urban Affairs Review* 31, no. 2 (November 1995).

Peterson, George E. "Urban Policy and the Cyclical Behavior of Cities." In *Reagan and the Cities,* edited by George E. Peterson and Carol W. Lewis. Washington, D.C.: Urban Institute Press, 1986.

Peterson, Paul E. *City Limits.* Chicago: University of Chicago Press, 1981.

Peterson, Paul E., and Mark C. Rom. *Welfare Magnets: A New Case for a National Standard.* Washington, D.C.: Brookings Institution Press, 1988.

Poole, Keith, and Howard Rosenthal. "Patterns of Congressional Voting." *American Journal of Political Science* 35, no. 1 (February 1991).

Putnam, Robert. "Tuning In, Tuning Out: The Strange Disappearance of Social Capital in America." *PS: Political Science and Politics* 28, no. 4 (December 1995).

Reagan, Ronald. *Public Papers of the Presidents of the United States: Ronald Reagan, 1982.* Vol. 1. Washington, D.C.: GPO, 1983.

Reich, Robert B. *Tales of a New America.* New York: Times Books, 1987.

———. "Succession of the Successful." *New York Times Magazine,* 20 January 1991.

Reinhold, Robert. "Chasing Votes from Big Cities to the Suburbs." *New York Times,* 1 June 1992, sec. A.

Rieder, Jonathan. *The Jews and Italians of Brooklyn against Liberalism.* Cambridge, Mass.: Harvard University Press, 1985.

Sandel, Michael J. *Democracy's Discontent: America in Search of a Public Philosophy.* Cambridge, Mass.: Harvard University Press, Belknap Press, 1996.

Savitch, H. V., David Collins, Daniel Sanders, and John P. Markham. "Ties That Bind: Central Cities, Suburbs, and the New Metropolitan Region." *Economic Development Quarterly* 7, no. 4 (November 1993).

Schneider, Mark. "The Progrowth Entrepreneur in Local Government." *Urban Affairs Review* 29, no. 2 (December 1993).

Schneider, Mark, and Thomas Phelan. "Black Suburbanization in the 1980s." *Demography* 30, no. 2 (May 1993).

Schneider, William. "The Suburban Century Begins: The Real Meaning of the 1992 Election." *Atlantic Monthly,* July 1992.

Schnore, Leo F. "The Socio-Economic Status of Cities and Suburbs." *American Sociological Review* 28, no. 1 (February 1963).

Schwartz, Barry, ed. *The Changing Face of the Suburbs.* Chicago: University of Chicago Press, 1976.

Sell, Ralph R. "Analyzing Migration Decisions: The First Step—Whose Decisions?" *Demography* 20, no. 3 (August 1983).

Skocpol, Theda. "Sustainable Social Policy: Fighting Poverty without Poverty Programs." *American Prospect* 1, no. 2 (summer 1990).

——. "A Partnership with American Families." In *The New Majority: Toward a Popular Progressive Politics*, edited by Stanley B. Greenberg and Theda Skocpol. New Haven: Yale University Press, 1997.

Stahura, John M. "Changing Patterns of Suburban Racial Composition, 1970–1980." *Urban Affairs Quarterly* 23, no. 3 (March 1988).

Stanback, Thomas M. Jr. *The New Suburbanization: Challenge to the Central City.* Boulder, Colo.: Westview Press, 1991.

Stein, Robert M. *Urban Alternatives: Public and Private Markets in the Provision of Local Services.* Pittsburgh: University of Pittsburgh Press, 1990.

"The Suburban Vote Conforming to What?" *The Economist,* 17 October 1992.

"Suburbia: A Republican Way of Life." *The Economist,* 11 May 1991.

"Suburbs: Potential but Unrealized House Influence." *Congressional Quarterly Weekly Report,* 6 April 1974.

Thomas, Evan, Karen Breslau, Debra Rosenberg, Leslie Kaufman, and Andrew Murr. *Back from the Dead: How Clinton Survived the Republican Revolution.* New York: Atlantic Monthly Press, 1997.

Tiebout, Charles. "A Pure Theory of Local Expenditures." *Journal of Political Economy* 64, no. 5 (October 1956).

U.S. Department of Commerce, Bureau of the Census, *1990 Census of Population. General Population Characteristics. Metropolitan Areas.* Washington, D.C.: GPO, November 1992.

U.S. Department of Commerce, Bureau of the Census, *1990 Census of Population. Social and Economic Characteristics.* Washington, D.C.: GPO, 1993.

U.S. Department of Commerce, Bureau of the Census, *1990 Census of Population and Housing. Supplementary Reports.* Washington, D.C.: GPO, December 1993.

Warner, Sam Bass. *Streetcar Suburbs: The Process of Growth in Boston, 1870–1900.* Cambridge, Mass.: Harvard University Press, 1962.

Weir, Margaret. "Poverty, Social Rights, and the Politics of Place." In *European Social Policy: Between Fragmentation and Integration,* edited by Stephen Leibfried and Paul Pierson. Washington, D.C.: Brookings Institution Press, 1995.

———. "Is Anybody Listening? The Uncertain Future of Welfare Reform in the Cities." *Brookings Review* 15, no. 1 (winter 1997).

Whyte, William H. Jr. *The Organization Man.* New York: Simon and Schuster, 1956.

Wilson, William Julius. *The Truly Disadvantaged: The Inner City, the Underclass, and Public Policy.* Chicago: University of Chicago Press, 1987.

———. *When Work Disappears: The World of the New Urban Poor.* New York: Vintage Books, 1997.

Wirt, Frederick M., Francine Rabinowitz, Benjamin Walter, and Deborah Hensler. *On the City's Rim: Politics and Policy in Suburbia.* Lexington, Mass.: D.C. Heath, 1972.

Wolman, Harold, and Lisa Marckini. "Changes in Central-City Representation and Influence in Congress Since the 1960s." *Urban Affairs Review* 34, no. 2 (November 1998).

Woo, Michael. "Teaching about Cities." *Institute of Politics Newsletter* (fall/winter 1993–94).

Wood, Robert C. *Suburbia: Its People and Their Politics.* Boston: Houghton Mifflin, 1958.

Woodward, Bob. *The Agenda.* New York: Simon and Schuster, 1994.

Zikmund, Joseph II. "A Comparison of Political Attitude and Activity Patterns in Central Cities and Suburbs." *Public Opinion Quarterly* 31, no. 1 (spring 1967).

———. "Suburban Voting in Presidential Elections." *Midwest Journal of Political Science* 12, no. 2 (May 1968).

———. "Suburbs in State and National Politics." In *The Urbanization of the Suburbs,* edited by Louis H. Masotti and Jeffrey K. Hadden. Beverly Hills, Calif.: Sage Publications, 1973.

Index

DATE			